praise for RESOLVE

"Highly recommended reading for anyone who wants to bring their boldest, best self to conflict or negotiations."

AMY CUDDY, bestselling author of *Presence*

"*Resolve* has great stories, deep insights, and wise advice about how to solve conflicts with confidence. This book will change your life."

TIMOTHY D. WILSON, author of *Redirect*

"A useful guide for negotiating life's more difficult conflicts."

**JOHN GOTTMAN, PH.D., bestselling author of
*The Seven Principles for Making Marriage Work***

"So empowering, and not just for businesspeople.
This is a book for you and me."

DAR WILLIAMS, musician, writer

"Who among us would not benefit from approaching conflict and negotiations with greater confidence? That's what makes *Resolve* such an insightful and thought-provoking read. Hal Movius has helped countless individuals – and many of the world's largest multinationals – to be smarter and more effective in dealing with differences. Here are the tools and techniques that show us how."

**ALEXANDER GREEN, *New York Times* bestselling
author of *The Gone Fishin' Portfolio***

"In *Resolve*, Hal Movius gives us lively hands-on guidance for navigating our most stressful interpersonal encounters. His empowering voice should guide our country's and the world's statesmen and stateswomen as they tackle, rather than avoid, our pressing challenges."

**THE HONORABLE SARAH BLOOM RASKIN,
Deputy Secretary of the U.S. Department of the Treasury**

"Hal Movius has done a brilliant job of pulling together what psychology can teach us about how to raise our confidence level as a negotiator. Even the most reluctant and timid negotiators will benefit from his advice and coaching."

LAWRENCE SUSSKIND, vice-chair, Program on Negotiation at Harvard Law School

"When is the last time a business book was a page-turner? *Resolve* is just that: advice on how to become an all-around better negotiator, sprinkled with relevant real-life vignettes that bring it all home."

SUSAN SILBERMANN, senior life sciences executive

"*Resolve* dives headlong into the role of confidence in negotiations and leaves you with a very fresh perspective of the process. Movius explores common behavioral traps, mental minefields, and tricky situations that can trip up even the most seasoned negotiator. An entertaining and incredibly informative read for anyone in the field."

FRANCESCA GINO, Professor, Harvard Business School

"Having worked with Hal Movius on projects around the globe, I have witnessed firsthand how the practical insights in *Resolve* can help senior managers negotiate deals and disputes more effectively."

GUHAN SUBRAMANIAN, Professor, Harvard Law and Business Schools

"*Resolve* is an insightful and essential resource for anyone negotiating conflicts across differences of race, gender, and culture in the global marketplace."

MARTIN N. DAVIDSON, Professor, Darden Graduate School of Business, author of *The End of Diversity as We Know It*

"In his wise and empowering new book, *Resolve*, Hal Movius shows how genuine assurance arises from a rich fusion of mastery, awareness, and poise – all of which can be nurtured through honest reflection and diligent practice. Simply put, for us to perform at our best, we have to be at our best. With warm and sympathetic coaching, Movius shows us how to achieve that state."

MICHAEL WHEELER, Harvard Business School, author of *The Art of Negotiation*

NEGOTIATING
LIFE'S CONFLICTS
WITH GREATER
CONFIDENCE
RESOLVE

HAL MOVIUS

Published by
LifeTree Media Ltd.
www.lifetreemedia.com

Distributed by
Greystone Books Ltd.
www.greystonebooks.com

Cataloguing data available from Library and Archives Canada
ISBN 978-1-928055-23-5 (hardcover)
ISBN 978-1-928055-24-2 (epub)
ISBN 978-1-928055-25-9 (pdf)

Editing by Maggie Langrick
Copyediting by Audrey McClellan
Proofreading by Shirarose Wilensky
Jacket design by Peter Cocking
Interior design by Naomi MacDougall
Printed and bound in Canada by Friesens
Distributed in the U.S. by Publishers Group West

For my mother, Katherine

Contents

Acknowledgments

SIX YEARS ago, Roy Lewicki, Max Bazerman, Jared Curhan, and Mike Wheeler offered me brief but important feedback and direction on the topic of confidence in negotiations. Josh Weiss was an early thought partner; Marshall Hanbury, Saba Chinian, and Nik Sandev contributed their time during the research stage. Joanna Chango, Dan Wilson, Dar Williams, Bob Hower, Kira Hower, Geoffrey Movius, and David Finn shared ideas and support in long conversations. I thank all of them.

I'm deeply indebted to Jim Coan not only for his knowledge and insights, but also for his sense of humor and vulnerability. I thank Jacob Slichter, wise man and writing coach extraordinaire, for timely encouragement and feedback. My deep appreciation to Jerry Clore and Tim Wilson for their generous help and feedback at different stages.

Thank you to my gifted colleagues and partners at Movius Consulting, particularly to Larry Susskind, Guhan Subramanian, and David Fairman, from whom I have learned so much over the years. Thank you, Ellen Wingard, Rob Berkley, and Ondine Norman, for your support. Thanks also to the Consensus Building Institute; to CorpU; to my colleagues in Asia, Latin America, and Europe; and to long-term clients. You are great teachers, all.

Heartfelt thanks to Maggie Langrick at LifeTree Media for her passion and acumen in guiding this book into existence. Maggie's vision, encouragement, tireless editing, and incisive criticism shaped it from start to finish. Audrey McClellan improved the manuscript with her careful copyedit. Paris Spence-Lang and Marijean Oldham have kept the book's audience in mind at all times. Thank you.

Thank you, close friends. You know who you are.

Finally, thank you, Kate, Luke, and Anya, for your love and patience. I love you more than there are stars.

Introduction

DO YOU love a good mystery?

My wife and I have watched so many episodes of crime dramas that I'm afraid to list them. We seem to specialize in British serials, which are grittier and more realistic. But Australian, American, Canadian, Swedish – we're not choosy. As long as there are good plots, good acting, and not too much violence, we're in.

That may sound like a strange place to start the introduction to a book about feeling more confident in how you resolve conflict. But the truth is, the genesis of this book was my desire to tackle a mystery, a series of nagging contradictions and clues that I couldn't get out of my head. Like the detective in a good mystery, I wanted answers, and I suspected that those answers might provide a great deal of comfort and benefit to other people.

I got into the field of conflict resolution because it seemed like a useful way to contribute to the world. After all, conflicts create misery everywhere, from war zones to boardrooms to living rooms. Having grown up as the peacemaker in a family with varied political and religious stripes, I felt suited for the field. And perhaps because I'm anxious by nature, I found it easy to be a listener – a habit that allowed more time with the girls on whom I had crushes, even if I had to listen to them talk about *their* crushes.

In any case, after following my heart in several other ways – hitchhiking around the world; playing in rock bands – I was lucky enough to land a job assisting a talented group of mediators working in the space between public agencies, corporations, scientists, angry citizens, and teams of aggressive attorneys. The job provided a close-up view of how intense and personal conflict can be, and what a huge difference a masterful mediator can make. Even twenty years ago it seemed clear that our world was going to become more politically polarized, and that mediators would need to understand what *really* mattered to people with different instincts. So I went to graduate school to study negotiation and explore the links between physiology, personality, and ideology.

I also underwent clinical training in psychology, spending thousands of hours learning to provide psychotherapy to individuals, couples, and families. Interestingly, it became clear that psychologists themselves were embroiled in a huge dispute about which psychotherapies worked well, and which were less effective. The mentors I found were skeptical that any one approach had all the answers.

Having finished graduate school and clinical training, I embarked on a new career training leaders and teams to communicate and negotiate more effectively. At first it was a thrill just to receive a written evaluation afterward with high ratings and nice comments. But after awhile, curiosity set in. Did the training actually work? Did people change their behaviors as a result of what they had learned in the classroom? With the support of Larry Susskind and the Program on Negotiation at Harvard Law School, I spent a year researching and writing about the effectiveness of negotiation training. Larry and I then got much more curious about the barriers to change and wrote a book, *Built to*

Win, about how organizations can make it harder or easier for their people to negotiate well.

Which leads me back to the mystery.

For the last ten years I've been preoccupied with helping people to actually change their behaviors at the negotiating table. From hundreds of confidential interviews, I've learned that even among senior executives from sales and purchasing teams who negotiate for a living, negotiation is most often experienced as perilous and stressful. Even 40 years after the introduction of the phrase "win-win," most people find it hard to walk out of a training session and into a negotiation where they find themselves using a more constructive, problem-solving approach.

Why?

The answer most often mentioned by clients and students: *confidence*. If only it didn't wilt in the face of difficult counterparts. If only I had the guts to confront the colleague who is annoying me. If only I had been as confident in the actual negotiation as I was when preparing for it. And if only I could negotiate with my sister/spouse/kids the way I negotiated that deal last week!

This honesty from clients has caused me to reflect on my own experience. If I felt comfortable coaching teams in high-stakes negotiations during the day, why was it that arguments with my kids about bath time could turn me from Dr. Jekyll into Mr. Hyde? Why were certain people and situations especially stressful? Why couldn't I always convert the knowledge and strategies I knew inside out into the perfect problem-solving words in my own stressful situations?

I wrote to colleagues in the academic world and asked, "What does research tell us about the effect of confidence on negotiating? Can we teach confidence? Should we?" Many wrote thoughtful responses, noting plentiful research on the ways in which cognitive biases and limitations can worsen and prolong disputes. If anything, they suggested, teaching people to be more confident might make things *worse*! But a few colleagues suggested that while we knew a lot about the mental mistakes that people make in conflicts, that might not be the whole story about confidence.

And that's when the mystery really took shape, coalescing into three questions:

1. What does it mean to be "confident" in approaching a conflict or negotiation?
2. Does confidence help or hinder us?
3. Is confidence something that can be learned, and if so, how?

This book is my attempt to answer that mystery and these questions. (Spoiler alert: confidence *does* help, and it *can* be learned.) I've spent two years reviewing more than a thousand studies and translating the findings into usable advice.

Even if you are a highly capable and successful person, you are not alone in wanting to avoid or move quickly through conflict. Even if you negotiate for a living, or have been to negotiation courses – or teach them (*ahem!*) – you're not crazy if you find it really hard to put new ideas and intentions into practice at the negotiating table. In the coming pages I'll help explain why this is, and what you can do about it.

In Chapter 1, I'll explain why conflict can feel so perilous, how we usually deal with it, and why negotiation is very often the most powerful approach to resolving it well. In Chapter 2, I'll draw on 40 years of research to provide an overview of what makes a good – and a great – negotiator. I'll also show you how to turn conflict into an opportunity to negotiate, which is sometimes the hardest move.

In Chapters 3, 4, and 5, I'll describe how you can build *mastery*, *awareness*, and *poise*, the three components of confidence that can change how you act, think, and feel as you approach and navigate conflicts and negotiations.

In Chapters 6, 7, and 8, I'll help you apply your new understanding of confidence to three special situations: dealing with tough tactics, negotiating when the relationship is paramount, and negotiating on behalf of others.

Simply reading a book is no guarantee that you'll wake up six months from now and find you're negotiating with less stress and better results – much as I wish that were the case. Becoming a more confident negotiator begins with new insights, but as with any complicated activity, success requires practice. Chapter 9 is all about *you*; with the Appendix, it provides tools to help you understand your own tendencies, and shows how to use what you've learned from these pages to tackle your own challenges.

I know personally how easy it is to feel stymied by the prospect of negotiating, how angry and anxious we can become after dealing with difficult people or behaviors, and how disproportionately dreadful conflict can be when we're in it with close friends or family members.

In some ways, it reminds me of an old joke:

A guy goes to a psychiatrist and says, "Doc, my brother's crazy; he thinks he's a chicken."

The doctor says, "A chicken? How long has he been this way?"

"Six months."

"Really? Why didn't you bring him in sooner?"

"I would have, but we needed the eggs."

We do need the eggs: we can't live without other people. Relationships are critical to our health, our happiness, and our ability to get things done in the world. But we don't need to live with our own improvised patterns and solutions in the face of conflict.

This book is meant to give you the ideas and tools you need to launch your own personal practice of influence and negotiation. You can become more confident in three critical ways and thereby change the way that you resolve differences in your own life, at home and at work. You may not believe it now, but by the end of our journey together, I hope to persuade you that learning to negotiate with greater confidence may be the single most valuable investment in yourself – and your relationships – that you can make.

Ready?

"With confidence, you have won before you have started."

—MARCUS GARVEY

CHAPTER 1

The Crucible and the Catalyst

Why conflict is hard, and how confidence can help

CONFLICT IS an inescapable fact of life. When philosopher Jean-Paul Sartre opined that "hell is other people," that's what he was getting at. (Probably not the best roommate, Sartre.) People around us sometimes do annoying things, and we apparently do things that annoy them, too. We argue with friends, family, and colleagues about whose beliefs are valid, whose predictions will prove correct, and which values and principles should apply to a problem or situation.

While debating or arguing can sometimes be fun, more often it's stressful. In fact, research reveals that among all the daily stressors we experience, the worst by far is interpersonal conflict.[1] On a scale of pleasant-to-unpleasant experiences, people rate interpersonal conflict on a par with having their car break down in traffic, sleeping on an airport floor, or sitting through a long, hot funeral.[2] Conflict – or the prospect of it – can hijack our thoughts and feelings for hours, days, and sometimes much longer. Consider Karen's situation, for example:

THINGS HAVE been going pretty well for Karen in her new job. After nearly a year she still likes the atmosphere, people, and challenges of a small start-up. But lately there have been some bumps in the road. Work-from-home Fridays were abandoned last month after too many people goofed off. Last week her boss, Alex, asked her to move to a cubicle next to two of the loudest people in the office. And yesterday she discovered that the newest hire had been offered a salary higher than hers. These developments have been gnawing at her – particularly the salary. It feels as though management's attitude has changed. Or maybe they have been fooling her all along?

"They must think I'm a sucker," she fumes to a friend after work.

The friend tells her, "You need to stand up for your rights! Tell them what you have to have, or else you're leaving!"

I'm not so sure I should do that, she thinks. *I don't want to come across as aggressive. I really like this job.* She wants to ask Alex for a month off next summer to travel with a friend; getting pushy about her salary and work conditions might not help with that. She imagines Alex scowling or scolding her, or simply thinking of her as selfish and demanding. She shudders.

"I hate negotiations!" she posts on social media. The replies and suggestions are all over the map. One person posts a picture of an elephant charging, with the caption *Get Tough.* But many others echo her feelings: "me too" and "the worst."

Now Karen is lying awake at 3:23 a.m., thinking about what to say and do. *I want to be seen as a team player,* she thinks, *not a prima donna.* Alex is likable, and a good mentor. But this move to the cubicle: What does it mean? And the salary: What should she ask for? Should she reveal that she knows about the new person's higher salary? That might backfire . . . Should she

threaten to leave? Submit a list of demands? Her thoughts are racing as she feels a knot forming in her stomach.

Conflict can produce some of life's most anxiety-provoking experiences. Even the most powerful people among us feel less capable coping with conflict than they would wish. When Stanford Business School surveyed 200 North American CEOs, managing conflict was the most commonly cited problem for which they wanted help.[3] I've asked thousands of leaders the question *How many of you truly like to negotiate?* Across more than two dozen countries and hundreds of organizations, the result is always the same: very few hands go up.

Why is conflict so difficult to manage? Why is negotiation so daunting? One reason is that there's usually more at stake than we realize.

THE CONFLICT CRUCIBLE

When we're in conflict with another person, we're typically trying to manage up to three different problems.

1. **Achieving our material goals.** These goals focus on achieving the tangible results we want out of a situation: we want to secure benefits and minimize risks or costs. While material goals are often financial in nature, they can also include desired experiences, goods, services, or policies. Material goals can include:

- The terms of exchange, as in a purchase or sale
- Access to resources, as in use of the car on Thursday night
- Compensation for harm, as in settling a claim
- Shared decisions, as in how to spend a family vacation
- A process or method for reaching a solution or making a decision

Like the tip of an iceberg, material goals are the visible objects of discussion. But two other goals lie just under the surface of most conflicts and can make them far more difficult to navigate.

2. **Building social capital.** Humans are intensely social animals; even the most introverted person must sometimes depend physically, emotionally, socially, and materially on others in order to survive and thrive. The term *social capital* reflects the idea that we have earned the trust and good will of others, and can draw on it in the future. Having good relationships and a good reputation with others not only helps us achieve our material goals more effectively over time; it has also been shown to reduce stress and illness.[4] Conflicts are stressful in part because they put our social capital at risk.[5]

3. **Managing emotion.** Trying to get what we want while preserving social capital is hard enough. But a third challenge can get thrown in at any moment: the hot potato of negative emotion. Anxiety, anger, guilt, disappointment . . . negative emotions like these can derail us from our pursuit of material and social goals. As we will see in Chapter 5, some of us are generally more prone than others to experiencing negative emotion. We also vary in how we cope with emotions – and when it comes to conflict, some ways work better than others.

Not all conflicts are alike, and material, social, and emotional goals are not always equally important from one situation – or person – to the next. But these three kinds of goals form what I call *the conflict crucible*. A crucible can be defined in two ways: a container or environment in which ingredients interact intensely and can be transformed; or a difficult test or ordeal. (The original medieval Latin word *crucibulum* referred to a night lamp that illuminated the darkness.)

The conflict crucible is a metaphor for the complex and sometimes intense mixture of elements that are at stake when we seek to resolve conflict. Conflict puts us under pressure, but can also produce new and beneficial outcomes when we deal with it wisely.

Negotiation is a powerful strategy for dealing with conflict. We'll learn much more about it in Chapters 2 and 3. Yet three other strategies are more commonly used to deal with conflict, and it's important to understand why we use them so often and why they may not always serve us well.[6]

Avoidance and giving in

"Ever make it through a week without a rationalization?" a character asks in the movie *The Big Chill*. In the service of avoiding conflict, we all rationalize like crazy. We downplay our own goals ("I didn't really care about that anyway"). We disengage from relationships when they become stressful ("Okay, whatever; I'll find someone else"). We ignore messages, or delay responding to requests. We post criticisms online anonymously, or gossip about others rather than confronting them directly. We point to rules, regulations, or authorities and say, "Sorry, I had no choice." We pretend to agree with a decision but then undermine it, or resist going along with it.

A close cousin of avoidance is giving in: we engage with (rather than avoid) the other person, but end up agreeing to most or all of their requests.[7]

Avoiding and giving in are more common strategies than you might think. In fact, it might sound like a bold claim, but avoiding conflict is probably the default mode for most people. Research has shown that when we expect to deal with a competitive person, we believe we will behave more competitively. Yet when the moment arrives, we actually give in more easily – becoming *less* competitive, setting lower aspirations, and eventually settling for less.[8]

It's not a new insight. More than eighty years ago, sociologist Richard LaPiere traveled around the United States for two years with a Chinese couple, noting that they were refused service at only one hotel out of sixty-six. But when the same hotels were later asked in a mail survey whether they would accept Chinese guests, 92 percent replied that they would not.[9] The lesson? People don't always behave the way they say they will.

Two other classic lines of research, carried out by psychologists Stanley Milgram and Solomon Asch, show that humans give in to others more often than we might believe. Milgram had subjects administer brief shocks to a person they believed was a fellow subject whenever that person made an error on a learning task. (In reality no one was being shocked.) Obeying the experimenter, two-thirds of the subjects eventually administered what they believed to be fatal shocks, although it evidently caused many of them great distress to do so. Asch had subjects join a group – actually his confederates – to supposedly complete studies on perception. Asch's confederates had been instructed to give obviously incorrect answers. Yet most of the time subjects gave the same answer as the group, to avoid being in conflict with them. (Interestingly, subjects were much braver when there was one other person who spoke up, contradicting the group; having a little social capital makes it easier to take risks.)

The conflict crucible helps us understand why: avoidance and giving in both reflect the hidden pull of our social and emotional goals.[10] We worry that speaking up will damage our connection with other people or their opinion of us, or produce emotional distress. As a consequence, we often simply do whatever it takes to avoid conflict with those around us, particularly peers or superiors. We don't want to risk losing social capital or feeling bad. In some cultures – and families and organizations – preserving outward harmony is an especially important value, one that makes avoidance and giving in the dominant short-term strategies for dealing with conflict. And at the individual level, some of us tend to give in more readily than others, a tendency that is partly heritable.[11]

There are times when avoidance or giving in can be the right approach. Sometimes avoided conflicts resolve themselves when issues or moods pass, plans or priorities change, or new options unfold. And giving in can make sense when the issues or outcomes matter far more to the other person than to us, or when the other person has more power than we do. But avoiding and giving in too often will make it harder for us to achieve our material goals in the long run. Although we may feel better and avoid social friction in the short term, habitually acting to escape or avoid conflict also means that we miss opportunities to deepen relationships and create more satisfying emotional experiences through problem solving.

Influence strategies

When we want something and believe that others might stand in our way, a common move is to try to influence them to accept our idea or proposal. Influence can involve an array of tactics that range in levels of assertiveness or aggression, as shown in Figure 1.

Least aggressively, we can plead with other people, appealing to their sense of fairness or compassion. We can suggest options that would benefit us. We can marshal arguments, pointing to sources of information or principles that bolster our case. We can use incentives, offering rewards or benefits for doing what we want, or creating costs or penalties if they don't change their position. As we move into costs and penalties, though, we stand at the cusp of coercion, which is the use of influence strategies that compel others to give in, even if they don't want to.

FIGURE 1

INFLUENCE TACTICS

LESS AGGRESSIVE	MORE AGGRESSIVE
Pleading . . . Suggestions . . . Arguments . . . Incentives . . . Threats . . . Force	
PERSUASION	COERCION

Coercion can take the form of threats: we promise or suggest undesirable consequences for the other person or group if they won't do what we want. Most aggressively, we can use force to compel others to do as we wish. (The use of force may violate your values as well as the law; it burns social capital and often begets physical resistance or violence. Therefore, my own rule of thumb is that we should only resort to force to resolve conflicts when someone's actions create imminent harm to us or to someone else, and no other action seems likely to prevent that harm.[12])

The appropriateness and effectiveness of influence tactics depends heavily on the nature of the relationship between the people involved, their relative power, and cultural norms. As we move from left to right along the continuum of tactics, social capital and emotional harmony become harder to preserve. Moreover, even if we don't care much about emotions or relationships, resorting to influence strategies too often and too quickly may make life harder over time. Why? In the short term, pushing for what we want can cause others to dig in their heels and respond in kind, pushing for *their* preferred options. The risk of impasse grows, as well as the risk of a long, inefficient process for reaching a solution. In the longer term, pushing for what we want leaves us with a reputation for selfishness. We lose social capital, and it becomes harder to achieve our goals with and through other people.

Compromise

A third common response to conflict is to seek compromise: each side gives a little, sacrificing some part of their own desired outcome for the sake of reaching an agreement. Most cultures teach children to compromise from an early age. Taking turns, sharing, and dividing up a resource or opportunity are all rituals that reflect the spirit of compromise, harnessing what seems to be a hardwired instinct in all primates: reciprocity.[13] Compromise makes sense when we need to get something agreed quickly. It is the most common strategy for *satisficing*, a term coined by Nobel Prize winner

Herbert Simon that means finding a "good enough" solution rather than the perfect one.[14]

Yet when the material stakes are high, compromise can be a costly and inefficient way to resolve differences. For example, imagine two friends who have decided to be roommates. Terri desperately wants to live near the city center, and she's willing to pay a higher rent to do that. Paula has financial constraints and is less put off by living farther out of town. Terri and Paula ultimately decide to compromise on both location and price: they find a place slightly out of town that is a little more than Paula would like to pay. But now neither is happy.

Compromise can also feel morally unacceptable when values are at stake. "How about you steal from me less often?" or "What if we only pollute half the pond?" are not solutions that people can live with – or should. Cutting-the-baby-in-half options are not going to generate wise or stable agreements.

Negotiation

Negotiation is a process through which people with conflicting views and goals voluntarily communicate with one another to try to reach an agreement that satisfies both sides' most important needs.[15]

Note these elements:

- There are at least *some* differences in what the parties want or believe.
- No one is imposing terms on the parties; they are seeking agreement voluntarily.
- The parties are dealing with a decision or the terms of an exchange (most typically, money exchanged for goods or services).

Unlike avoidance and giving in, negotiation focuses hard on meeting our most important needs – or at least, that's what it should do. While influence plays a part in most negotiations, it is fundamentally a one-way street: one person or group wants to convince or change another. Negotiation is a two-way street: it acknowledges that people arrive with different preferences and assumptions, and it searches for ways to deal with those differences. Unlike compromise, negotiation doesn't suggest meeting halfway, or sacrificing material goals right out of the gate for the sake of the relationship. When done well, it can create better solutions than compromising would, by generating options that give each side more of what they value most.

Think back to the roommates introduced earlier: a negotiated solution might have resulted in Terri paying 60 percent of the rent and taking the bigger bedroom in an apartment near the city center, so that she and Paula could live where Terri preferred *and* stay within Paula's budget. That solution is more efficient than a result achieved through compromise, because each roommate gives something that is less important to her, in exchange for something she deems more important.

With so much to be gained from negotiating, why don't we turn to it more often?

One reason is that we don't learn it early enough, or from good role models. We watch our parents, siblings, friends, neighbors, and teachers deal with conflict situations, usually defaulting to influence strategies (pleas, arguments, threats), avoidance ("I can't deal with this; I'm going out for a walk now"), or compromise (like taking turns or splitting something in half). We simply don't see good negotiation modeled often enough.

A second reason is that negotiating is a complicated activity, like learning a musical instrument or the skills of a sport. Even when we have been exposed to new ideas about negotiation, perhaps through training programs or coaching, it can be hard to apply what we have learned. It's not just that old habits die hard – which is true – but that our new, improved ideas and practices can run straight into barriers created by those around us. (Larry

Susskind and I wrote about the ways in which negotiators are thwarted by their own organizations, and what to do about it, in *Built to Win: Creating a World-Class Negotiating Organization*.)

But there is a third factor that looms largest: confidence. It's the critical ingredient we can add to our conflict crucible – a catalyst that accelerates and improves results.

DEFINING CONFIDENCE

Take a moment to think of two people in your life: one who seems comfortable dealing with difficult people and situations, and one who does not. As you compare them, you might begin to make the kinds of intuitive distinctions shown in Table 1.

TABLE 1

WHAT DOES IT MEAN TO BE CONFIDENT?

CONFIDENT	NOT CONFIDENT
Engages	Avoids
Calm, focused	Nervous, distracted
Clear	Confused, ambivalent
Speaks up; assertive	Afraid to speak up; a pushover
Knows what to do	Isn't sure what to do
Monitors the situation	Monitors own thoughts, feelings
Asks insightful questions	Is afraid to ask questions
Optimistic; sees possibilities for good outcomes	Resigned or vigilant; doesn't expect good outcomes
Looks forward to learning from others in interactions	Worries about being dominated or exploited by others
Acts	Reacts

Table 1 describes some intuitive distinctions we might make, but these aren't the whole story.

11

Most of us would like to spend more time in the left column. Wouldn't life be easier? But as you look at these two lists, you probably place yourself somewhere in between.

According to Merriam-Webster's dictionary, *confidence* is a feeling or belief that we can do something well. In more technical terms, confidence represents our attitude toward our ability to perform well in a specific situation or context. (Social psychologists have previously focused on attitudes as having affective, behavioral, and cognitive components, a useful framework upon which I draw here.)

Confidence is not the same as self-esteem

Self-esteem is a general evaluation or feeling about our overall worth as a person, yet it's only moderately related to our sense of effectiveness in any particular activity.[16] For example, Steve might feel fairly good about himself generally but lack confidence as a hockey player, singer, or negotiator (particularly around his older brother, who is good at those things). Maia suffers from low self-esteem but feels commanding and relaxed when she sits down at the piano to play Chopin. Global feelings of worth probably help us have positive expectations about social situations, but our confidence in ourselves is specific to particular situations and tasks.

Confidence and competence don't always go together

We tend to think of confidence as something that comes naturally with talent or skill. Sometimes – but not always – it does indeed work out that way.

Jeff Evans was the sports information director at Arizona State when Dustin Pedroia, now a major league all-star, showed up to baseball camp as a college freshman. In a 2015 interview with ESPN's Gordon Edes,[17] Evans recalled Pedroia's incongruous bravado on that late summer day in Tempe.

At 5′9″ inches tall and then an estimated 138 lbs, Pedroia was far from physically imposing. As the baby-faced 18-year-old swaggered onto the field, Evans said, "I look at Graham Rossini, our director of baseball operations, and I say, 'That's Pedroia?'"

Most new recruits would probably experience jitters on their first practice day, but if Pedroia was nervous, it didn't show. He marched right up to Evans, flexed his biceps, and asked, "How do you like these guns?" Evans turned to Rossini and remarked, "Wow, it's going to be a fun three years."

Once the season started, Pedroia's theatrical displays of confidence became one of the most entertaining features of any Sun Devils game. "He'd come in and say, 'Laser show today, laser show today, I'm going to hit bombs today,' then he'd go out and do it," Evans said. "That's the way he carried himself, and it didn't stop."

Evans recalled a particular game in which Pedroia was up to bat against Jered Weaver, who was considered to be the best pitcher in the country. Pedroia hit a scorching line drive to third base. Evans noted, "On his way back to the dugout, he's yelling, 'We'll be here all day,' right at Weaver."

Pedroia turned out to be highly competent as well as confident; his all-star performance and commitment to team play over many years are what make his youthful boasts amusing now rather than obnoxious. Being able to draw on exceptional skills can boost confidence – that's the "mastery" component of confidence, which we'll get into in Chapter 3. But in negotiation, the two are not as tightly linked as we might think. For one thing, people aren't always good judges of their own abilities. Psychologists David Dunning and Justin Kruger found that the most *incompetent* people on particular tasks were also the least aware of it; their incompetence kept them from realizing how incompetent they were! [18] However, if we are less confident, we may achieve a very good result in a negotiation but continue to doubt ourselves long afterward because we felt anxious all the way through the process.

The added problem with negotiation is that it is hard to know how well we succeeded compared to what was possible. After Andrew Carnegie became the richest man in the world by selling his company to J.P. Morgan, Carnegie wondered aloud whether he should have asked for $100 million more. "If you had, you would have gotten it," Morgan replied.[19] But this is a rarity: the people we're negotiating with don't typically tell us afterward what was really possible. Even if they do, we can't be sure they are being honest. And even honest counterparts might have failed to think of options that could have left us both better off (like Terri and Paula's solution).

Confidence is not the same as assertiveness

It's important not to confuse confidence with self-promotion or pushiness. While Pedroia's trash-talking may have annoyed or unnerved opponents in sports arenas, effective negotiation requires a different approach. Telling counterparts that we are powerful or that they should do what we want is really just an attempt to persuade or coerce. It can only take us so far in negotiations, particularly if we value relationships and our reputation.

As we'll see, we can learn to be more confident *as ourselves*, rather than by mimicking more aggressive tactics. Sometimes being confident leads us to be assertive in our communication, but this is not its only effect. At other times it might lead us to acquire critical information, formulate solutions to the problem before us, or keep cool in the face of a belligerent counterpart.

Is it possible to be too confident?

You might be wondering: Is it wise to try to cultivate confidence? After all, many conflicts are worsened or prolonged by people who seem too stubborn or sure of themselves. Perhaps we should strive for *some* confidence, but not too much?

As we'll see in Chapter 4, research has shown that we do indeed tend to make predictable mistakes when we are negotiating, and are often overly confident that we are right. But when research psychologists speak about this kind of "overconfidence," they are talking about being overly certain in estimates or predictions.

Confidence as I'm defining it means feeling better able to deal with the task at hand. It's possible to feel quite confident (even *too* confident!) in our predictions of what someone will say or do, while at the same time being filled with anxiety and dreading the confrontation.

To get past this contradiction, we need to understand that confidence is not a matter of finding the "Goldilocks solution" (not too much or too little, but just the right amount). That's because confidence isn't one thing, but three.

A MULTIDIMENSIONAL VIEW OF CONFIDENCE

As we approach any complex task, including conflict, it's useful to understand confidence in terms of three distinct components.[20]

A behavioral component: Mastery

Behavioral confidence, or *mastery*, is knowing how to do something without having to think hard about it. A skier or race car driver has a sense of just how much pressure it will take to turn at an optimal angle on a particular course. A guitarist spontaneously makes interesting choices about the notes to play in a solo. A presenter feels comfortable taking questions that might lead in a number of unexpected directions, while still being able to keep the discussion focused on key insights and themes. We have mastered something when it becomes almost second nature to us.

Achieving mastery is aided by having a mental map, a set of steps we intend to take. For negotiation, we need a map that is flexible enough to address a variety of contexts. It should suggest key moves or behaviors that happen together or in a sequence. It should help us understand how and where things might be getting off track, and should show us how to reset or restart.

Mastery requires practice as well. We can learn how to do something complicated by watching others do it, particularly as we compare what they did to our mental map. But at some point we have to move beyond observation. If we want to become better swimmers, it might help to watch a video of someone swimming, but sooner or later we will have to jump in the pool.

A cognitive component: Awareness

Confidence also has a cognitive (thinking) component. When we find ourselves in conflict with others, our brain naturally wants to size up the situation quickly. *Am I right? Are they? Can I trust them? Is what they're proposing good or bad for me? Why are they acting this way? What should I say next?* In situations where our goals, relationships, and emotions are at stake, the brain takes all kinds of shortcuts to help us quickly make sense of what is happening and how best to respond. The limitations of intuitive thinking can skew our judgment, leading us to become not only overly optimistic about the accuracy of our assumptions and beliefs but also sometimes unnecessarily pessimistic in situations where we feel powerless.

The key to more effective thinking about conflict is to expand our *awareness*.[21] To be more confident that we're seeing situations and solutions wisely, we must supplement our brain's well-worn shortcuts (which serve us well in many situations) with tools that encourage us to use more systematic and deliberative thinking. When we lose our keys, we automatically search for them in the familiar places, almost without thinking. But if they don't turn up, we begin to think more systematically: *Where did I go today? Where could I have put them down?* Systematic thinking takes more effort, but can be crucial in getting us to a good outcome.

An emotional component: Poise

Finally, confidence has an emotional component, *poise*. This is a state in which we are aware of our thoughts and feelings but not driven by them. Poise allows us to focus productively as we prepare for, carry out, and reflect on a difficult exchange. It allows us to think more clearly and systematically during moments of conflict, and to perceive and acknowledge emotions in others without reacting too quickly to them. We feel alert, calm, ready, and curious rather than anxious, impatient, or defensive.

Anxiety is the great disruptor of poise. Feeling anxious makes us less able to imagine how problems and situations look to others.[22] It makes us less likely to ask questions and more likely to ramble on. It makes us less creative and patient in the face of obstacles. It can scramble our plans and ideas, sending us into loops of self-doubt and second-guessing. Most importantly, anxiety increases the chances that we will avoid negotiations and conflicts altogether rather than addressing them proactively.

CONFIDENCE IS A CATALYST FOR BETTER RESULTS

Thinking about confidence in terms of these three components points us toward better strategies for approaching the conflict crucible. This view of confidence helps us realize what we are really up against, and asks us to think in distinct ways about different opportunities for improvement. Cultivating mastery, awareness, and poise is a recipe for achieving consistently better material, social, and emotional outcomes.

Remember Karen, who has issues to discuss with her boss, Alex? She is worried about her own material outcome, which could involve a number of issues: salary, time off, office location, and Friday work flexibility. She is debating what kind of influence strategy to use in her upcoming conversation (*Should I get tough? If so, how?*), and she wonders whether she should give in or avoid some issues, like salary. Guided by intuition, her mind is jumping to all kinds of conclusions. Her feelings are mixed, and she's not sure how to act on them wisely.

Would confidence help Karen approach this situation more effectively? Almost certainly, if research is any guide.

Studies show that some negotiators do consistently better than others, and that confidence is the key. Analyzing 75 scientific studies of negotiation and individual differences (in emotion, motivation, abilities, and beliefs), psychologist Hilary Elfenbein concluded: "The strongest and most reliable predictors of negotiation performance are also the most open to personal change. Namely, positive expectations and comfort with negotiation consistently predict better performance."[23]

Psychologists Laura Kray and Michael Haselhuhn have found something similar. Testing what has recently been called *mindset*[24] – a belief that abilities are either fixed or changeable – they discovered that students who believed negotiation skills could be improved got better at negotiating over the course of fifteen weeks, while those who saw negotiating as a "born, not made," skill failed to improve.[25]

Gandhi once remarked: "Man often becomes what he believes himself to be. If I keep on saying to myself that I cannot do a certain thing, it is possible that I may end by really becoming incapable of doing it. On the contrary, if I have the belief that I can do it, I shall surely acquire the capacity to do it even if I may not have it at the beginning."

He was onto something. When it comes to dealing with conflict, we rely on intuition, lurch through feelings, and improvise strategies for influencing, avoiding, or compromising. But with greater confidence we can learn to use negotiation strategies more often and more effectively in a wide range of situations.

In the next chapter I'll describe the principles and practices of negotiation in more detail and explain what separates good negotiators from great ones. In Chapters 3 to 5, I'll explain how to develop *mastery*, expand your *awareness*, and summon *poise* as you prepare for and carry out negotiations.

My goal is to help you become more confident in dealing with conflict without becoming arrogant or foolish, or having to act like someone you are not. I'll draw on brilliant research from colleagues, on my training as a psychotherapist, and my own experience as teacher, coach, and consultant to leaders in more than 40 organizations across 30 countries.

Increasing your confidence as a negotiator can help you achieve better results, deepen and protect relationships, enhance your reputation, manage emotions more effectively, and increase your sense of well-being. (Won't that be great?)

And the first task is to learn more about what it takes to negotiate.

"We are going to have peace even if we have to fight for it."

—DWIGHT D. EISENHOWER

CHAPTER 2

From Conflict to Negotiation

Thinking like a great negotiator

ONE SUMMER afternoon many years ago, a colleague and I were stumped. The senior executive on the other end of the line was describing, in painful detail, the conflicts that arose repeatedly between two groups in his company. Each group had particular goals and priorities, which were not always perfectly aligned. Each group was trying to do what it thought best for the company.

"Maybe they need to negotiate more effectively," we suggested when he had finished.

There was a long pause. "Well, no. I don't think . . . I wouldn't want that. We have a collaborative culture here. We're partners. We work things out."

We tried again. "These two groups have somewhat different responsibilities and priorities within the business, right?"

"Yes."

"So they might disagree on what would be best for the company, but they're both trying to do what they see as most important for it?"

"That's right."

"And they don't need to negotiate?"

Another pause. "Again, I'd say we work things out together. Not always smoothly, of course."

What were we missing? After a few more calls it became clear: the organization's leaders didn't like the word *negotiate*. To them it suggested that something was wrong, or that people were thinking or acting selfishly.

This story illustrates some common misconceptions about what negotiation is, and what it takes to negotiate successfully. Many people still think of negotiation as a combative or manipulative undertaking, a special arena in which we have to set aside valued relationships and emotional harmony in order to get what we want. But expert negotiation doesn't have to be about manipulation or coercion, or require that we check our values at the door.

NEGOTIATION PRINCIPLES
AND PRACTICES

Thousands of case studies, books, and lab experiments collectively point us to where and how things tend to go wrong in conflicts and negotiations, and what people can do to proceed more effectively. The next few pages boil down a half century of research into a few key ideas and practices, so get ready for a fast pace. (If you have read books like *Getting to Yes*, *Bargaining for Advantage*, *3-D Negotiation*, or *Built to Win*, some of these key moves will be familiar. If you're encountering them for the first time, rest assured we'll return to them again in more detail in different parts of the book.)

Good negotiators approach negotiation with some key skills and habits.

Analyze the consequences of no agreement (CONA)

Before they get to the table, good negotiators try hard to understand what each side believes will happen for them if no decision is reached. Thinking about their CONA (the consequences of no agreement) is a prelude to identifying and enhancing their best alternative to a negotiated agreement (BATNA), the course they will pursue if agreement cannot be reached. (A BATNA may not always feel like a "best" alternative; sometimes it is the least undesirable or least risky one.) Thinking about each side's perceived CONA protects negotiators from being influenced by an extreme first offer,[1] guides them in setting targets or aspirations, and alerts them to gaps in their knowledge.

Think carefully about interests

Good negotiators also think hard about their interests, which are the goals and concerns that underlie their demands and arguments. With the conflict crucible in mind, note that interests can be material (e.g., get a good price), social (look competent to my friends or colleagues), and emotional (avoid being embarrassed or frustrated). Interests can focus on short-term or long-term time horizons, and on achieving positive outcomes or avoiding negative ones. Peter might tell his work colleagues, "I can't stay for that meeting; I have to be home by 5:30 p.m." But the reason he has to be home, the underlying interest, might be that he needs time to clean the house and pick up food before friends arrive for dinner.

Explaining his own interests could help Peter to be more creative and proactive, rather than just reacting with a position. For example, if his boss were willing to pay for a taxi home and for take-out food to be delivered, Peter might be able to stay for another 45 minutes and contribute to the meeting, while still hosting a great dinner.

Good negotiators also think about *others'* interests. Why do they want what they want? What is the underlying need or motivation? Peter might ask his boss or colleagues to explain why his presence at the meeting is important. If they want him to comment on an idea, perhaps he could do that by phone during the drive home. If they want him to meet a new client, maybe he could come to a breakfast the next day. Learning to think in terms of interests makes situations less positional and opens the door to more efficient solutions.

Claim value by framing arguments effectively

In cases where negotiators are prepared to push hard to get what they want (*claim value*), they can preserve social capital and prevent bad feeling by framing arguments to directly address or respond to the other person's *interests*. A husband planning a vacation with his wife could say, "Here's the best option – it has great surfing, which I love!" (His interest.) Or he could say, "You've said you want to really relax but have a good Internet connection. I think you might like this location because it meets those needs better than any other option we've looked at." (Her interests.) He can also frame the proposal or option in terms of a precedent ("The Smiths loved this place") or a principle to which they both subscribe ("Last summer we did what you wanted; this summer it's my turn to choose"). In short, good negotiators tailor the argument to the audience.

Finally, when it comes to making arguments, less is more: research reveals that a few clear, responsive arguments are more effective than a long list.[2]

So far, so good. As in, that's what *good* negotiators do. But what about *great* negotiators? More than anything, it comes down to four additional habits: creating value, reframing, adopting a learning mindset, and focusing on process.

Create value before claiming it

The idea of *creating value* can be difficult to grasp, but it refers to moves that generate joint gains or "make the pie bigger" before dividing it up in a negotiation. There is a three-step recipe that great negotiators use:

1. They **uncover what matters most** to each side by explaining their key interests and priorities, and discerning the other person's.

(I use the word *discern* because we can't always directly ask the people we're negotiating with, and even when we can, they won't always know or reveal what is most important to them.)

2. They **notice differences** – in what each side values most, what each side believes (regarding capabilities, for example, or what will happen in the future), and what each side is willing to risk.

3. They **invent options** that exploit differences to produce gains for both parties. This practice is truly what separates good negotiators from great ones. When each person gets more of what they value most, it improves material outcomes, preserves social capital, and eases emotional tension. You want soup because you feel like comfort food, while I want a steak because I need protein? No problem! We can make beef stew together. We can make trades across issues that we value differently, in which I give in more on things you value most if you will give in more on things I value most.

Creating value doesn't mean giving in. It has nothing to do with "being nice." In fact, great negotiators know that the best way to get to the upper right corner of the chart in Figure 2 is to work hard to meet their own interests and the other person's. Starting with influence tactics – pleading or arguing for a proposal – makes it more likely that counterparts will adopt the same tactic; if the negotiations continue this way, the two sides will end up in the lower left quadrant of the chart in Figure 2, squabbling over their small pie. It is more efficient to engineer the conversation toward an outcome that lands in the northeast quadrant, particularly when relationships matter.

It sounds simple, but it's hard. Why?

There is an inherent tension in most negotiations between working to *create value* by crafting options that might benefit both sides, and working to *claim value* by influencing the other side to agree to our preferred options. While we're exploring ways to give

FIGURE 2

VALUE CHART

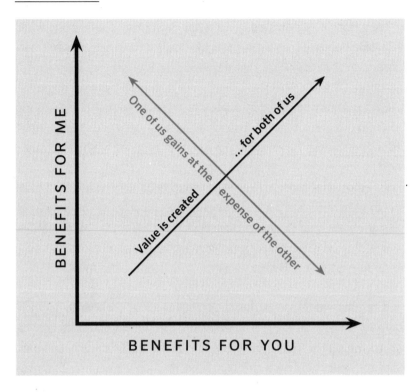

them more of what they want, we also need to be sure we're not leaving ourselves open to being exploited. If we are forthcoming and flexible and they are not, we could be taken to the cleaners. How can we get them to cooperate with us so that we can problem-solve together, without having to stick our neck out? That is the *Negotiator's Dilemma*.[3] Luckily, there are key process moves that foster value creation without taking unnecessary risks.

Propose solutions in packages

Rather than seeking to resolve one issue at a time, great negotiators think in terms of *packages*. If you and I haggle over each issue, ending up in the middle through compromise, the pie will never get bigger. For example, imagine we have four issues to discuss. The first one is most important to you, and the fourth one is most important to me. I could be more flexible on issue 1 if you could be more flexible on issue 4. Then perhaps we'd both feel more flexible about the remaining issues. But if we resolve the first issue – most important to you – only after a lot of haggling and compromise, you'll feel a lot less inclined to be flexible when it finally comes to my most important issue. We'll miss out on making a good trade.

Moreover, rather than creating one package, great negotiators try to create two or three, each of which is geared to meet different interests and priorities that their counterpart may have. A cable TV provider might offer different packages that vary the number of stations its subscribers receive, pricing the packages differently. Putting forward multiple packages that incorporate tradeoffs gives people choice, and increases the chance that the cable provider will learn more about what matters most to its customers.

Fractionate

To create value, great negotiators also know how to *fractionate* – to break one issue into several. They might take the issue of "how much to spend on a car" and divide it into a set of sub-issues: total budget, size of the down payment that's affordable, amount for a trade-in, and length and interest rate of the loan. Some of those issues might be more important to the car dealer (total price, length of loan); some more important to the buyer (down payment). Breaking down one big issue into several helps the buyer and seller make trades across things they value differently, rather than haggling over a single issue.

Offer concessions with conditions

Finally, when concessions (i.e., giving ground on some issues) are required to get a deal, great negotiators typically ask for something in return. "If I agree to your price, could we make it a two-year deal?" Or "How about I let you take the car for the weekend, and you pick up the tab for dinner next week?" Asking doesn't always mean the other side will comply, particularly if they have a very good BATNA to walk away to. But it is important to ask; there is little risk and often significant reward to be found, and it keeps the negotiations oriented toward further trades (creating value) rather than giving value away.

Reframe

Great negotiators excel at *reframing*, or recasting their views or arguments in a different light. When the other side criticizes our proposal, note their skepticism and suggest other options or ask questions to learn more. When someone threatens to walk away, acknowledge that as one option, but emphasize the benefits of continuing to work on a solution. Great negotiators reframe the other person's positions or demands in terms of the interests those demands are trying to meet.

Adopt a learning mindset

Great negotiators know that staying curious is a kind of super-power in negotiations. Curiosity alerts them to opportunities and prevents them from losing their cool in the face of tough tactics. They want to understand as much as possible about how their counterparts see the problem. They stay alert for new information or opportunities that emerge, and they ask questions to uncover any constraints or interests that are not immediately apparent. One study found that expert negotiators – those nominated by their peers as particularly good – spent 250 percent more time asking questions and listening than their peers in a control group.[4] Asking and listening helps uncover information that can lead to value-creating (and value-claiming) moves. In negotiations, information is power.

Focus on process

Great negotiators follow a process for managing the conversation.[5] They have a mental map of the stages that most negotiations go through. This map suggests specific tactics that might be important at each stage. It takes into account how much or how little time they have, and whether they will have opportunities to talk again with the person across the table. Most importantly, a mental map of where they plan to take the conversation helps to orient them (as good maps do). It helps them see when things are going off track or getting stuck, and suggests what they might do to get the discussion moving again in the right direction. (Chapter 3 will provide you with a general process map – Figure 3 – and more details about tactics that make sense at different stages of a negotiation.)

These are the practices that great negotiators bring to the table. But what if there is no table?

TRANSFORMING CONFLICTS INTO NEGOTIATIONS

When we have to make decisions that involve other people, or when we have things we want to trade or exchange, the table is fairly well set for a negotiation. But what about situations in which we're arguing over different beliefs or dealing with someone whose behavior is problematic? These kinds of conflicts are common, but they lead to negotiations less often. Before we know it, we get pulled into other habitual responses without considering negotiation as a strategy for resolving the conflict. Conflicts about beliefs and behaviors sometimes require set-up moves to create the opportunity to negotiate.

Conflicts about beliefs

No two people see the world in the same way. We may disagree over whose facts or sources are more accurate or relevant, what will happen in the future, or simply matters of taste. Sometimes our beliefs are based on deeply held values and moral instincts (for example, our view of the rightness or wrongness of the death penalty), which can inject deeply felt emotions and instincts into the conversation.

Of course, it can be entertaining and even educational to disagree and debate with others. When nothing is at stake (other than winning an argument), we are free to walk away, shaking our head at the other person's inability to see things our way. But when divergent beliefs make it harder to agree on a shared decision or transaction, three moves can help:

- **Joint fact-finding.** Rather than arguing over whether it is safe to swim in the local pond, we can agree to ask questions together, such as "How polluted is the pond?" and "Can people swim in it safely?" We then agree on sources of information that we both find credible and trustworthy – not your experts or friends, not mine. Joint fact-finding is now used in many policy settings to help resolve conflicts when there are sharply divergent beliefs about danger or risks, or about the effects or wisdom of possible solutions or policies.[6] Joint fact-finding isn't meant to provide a solution to the problem, but it can help create a common fact-based starting point from which to identify possible options, evaluate risks, and determine a course of action.
- **Help from third parties.** We can consult other people we both trust, or experts in a particular area (law, engineering, city planning, finance) to help us understand which facts are most relevant, how best to interpret those facts, and what future outcomes may be most likely. Sometimes (as in arbitration) we may agree ahead of time to live with whatever that third party or trusted authority decides.

- **Contingent agreements.** To handle a disagreement about the future, we can craft an agreement in the form of "if . . . then . . ." If prices *do* go up, then our deal is [X]. If they *don't*, then it is [Y]. Making bets is one kind of contingent agreement ("If the Cubs win, you pay me $100"), but we don't have to insist that one side wins and the other loses, necessarily.

Again, the key question is: Do our differing beliefs affect our ability to agree on a necessary or potentially beneficial decision or exchange? If so, the techniques above can help. If not, maybe *vive la difference!* is the best policy.

Conflicts about behavior

The roommate who keeps "borrowing" our food. The coworker's offensive comments. The loud talker broadcasting his least interesting thoughts on the train's quiet car. Regrettably, annoying or upsetting behaviors are a part of life. If we think these little frictions will pass, we choose avoidance, growling under our breath. But when the trespasses are more serious or persistent, we have to act.

> *BANG, BANG, BANG. Clang. Thud. Bang, bang, bang . . .*
>
> Dave can't believe it. For three days he has been woken by his new neighbor's roofing crew, pounding nails in the early dawn hours. The first day he merely moaned in the darkness, waiting for it to stop and assuming it was a one-time ordeal. When it resumed again the next morning he swore under his breath and vowed to take action. He left a short but firm note on the door: *Please ask the workers to start after 8:30 a.m.* Now, on the third morning, he is enraged. Throwing on pants, he runs downstairs and out the door, his heart pounding.
>
> "Hey!" he yells up to the neighbor's roof. "Hey!" The workers

stop for a moment. "You're not supposed to be out here so early. You're making too much noise!"

A large man, possibly the foreman, comes to the edge of the roof, shouting down a reply. "Sorry, but we've got to finish. We have other jobs to get to this week."

Dave feels his anger rising. "I left a note on the door! Didn't they tell you to come later?" A sense of futility and humiliation creeps over him. How could these people be such jerks?

"They're out of town," shouts the foreman.

"Well, you can't do this. I'm going to call the cops!" he shouts, striding back into his house.

Now he sits looking at the phone, his heart still racing. *Idiots!* he thinks. *Although maybe I'm being too hasty. Will calling the police make it worse?*

To deal with problematic behaviors, *influence* strategies are typically a first and necessary step to getting someone to negotiate with us. Potential customers won't want to discuss terms unless we first convince them that we have something they want or need. Roommates may not feel like altering their behavior until they sincerely understand that the status quo is unacceptable and needs to change.

Even though our ultimate aim is to resolve the problem, it can be difficult to raise an issue or confront a behavior when we fear rejection, disrespect, or humiliation. What if the other person says something like "You're crazy" or "That's not my problem"? What if they respond by threatening or insulting us? By ridiculing or ignoring us? Even the thought of these responses can be unnerving, pulling us toward avoidance. At these moments, we need to summon confidence. There are four powerful ways to do it.

1. **Connect with a friend.** Our brain and body will calm down a lot if we have someone to vent to and confide in, and who can

provide some sympathy and reassurance.[7] Sometimes all we need is to hear our friend say, "Wow, that's terrible! I would be so angry!" When someone validates our feelings, it helps us calm down and think. Dave calls his friend Al and explains what has happened. Al commiserates and helps him brainstorm. Already, Dave feels calmer.

2. **Think of a Plan B.** How might we get what we need through another course of action? If the roofers can't be stopped, can Dave sleep downstairs, in a quieter room, with headphones? Or get the phone number for the place where the vacationing neighbors are staying? Coming up with a backup plan (even a mediocre one) before approaching our counterpart will help us feel more powerful.

3. **Plan a constructive confrontation.** Here's the crux of it: How can we influence the other side so that they are willing to deal with us and address the problem at hand? Often, our strong emotions lead us straight to arguments, threats, or worse. When it comes time to engage, the following three moves can help steer things in the right direction:

- **Open with appreciation.** "I can see you guys are really busy," Dave might say, "and I'm sure you want to make progress."
- **Follow with a clear and specific complaint.** Even when we mean well, it is easy, when we are irritated by someone else, to criticize *the person* rather than complaining about *the behavior.* For example, Dave might be tempted to say something like "You may not be aware that this is a residential area." Even if he says it nicely, notice that it suggests the problem is the roofer's lack of awareness rather than the noise the crew is making. As we'll see in Chapter 6, criticism

sends conversations and negotiations in the wrong direction. He would be better off to simply say, "I work late, and this noise is making it impossible for me to sleep."

- **Suggest a solution – and ask for theirs.** "My thought is that maybe you could start a half hour later, or delay the banging until 7:00 and do other work on the house. What do you think? Is there a better solution?"

It is amazing how many times we discover that other people actually respond to these first three moves constructively, defying our fears. Sometimes, though, they won't be constructive. They will ignore, dismiss, or belittle our requests or suggestions. So we need to be prepared to do one more thing.

4. **Develop a "game-changing move."** It's useful to have another influence strategy in our back pocket if more cooperative moves don't work. Can we reward our counterparts for engaging with us? "Tell you what," Dave might say, "if we can come up with a plan to deal with the noise, I'll bring your crew a case of beer this afternoon." But what if the foreman is still unmoved? Dave might need to create a credible negative consequence. "Look," he might say, "if you're not willing to talk about this, then I really have no other choice but to call the zoning commission and the police department. I don't want to do that, and I'll bet we can work something out. But if I have to call them, I will."

Making threats about negative consequences is a stressful option for most of us. But notice that if we've done all the other things outlined here, it becomes far less daunting. We're already well into a conversation, even if it is not yet fruitful, and we're likely to feel less shaky and defensive as a result.

FROM KNOWLEDGE TO MASTERY

In this chapter, we've covered a lot of ground, looking at the things that good negotiators do, the extra skills that great negotiators apply, and the ways we can transform conflicts about beliefs and behaviors into negotiations. I hope you have a sense now for how and why negotiation can be so powerful, and what it takes to move from conflict to the negotiating table. But if you're feeling slightly bewildered, don't despair: we've covered 40 years of negotiation theory and research in only a few pages. It's time to look more concretely at how we can develop mastery, awareness, and poise at the negotiating table.

The real fun's about to begin.

"It's what you learn after you know it all that counts."

—KIN HUBBARD

CHAPTER 3

Mastery

Building confidence in our skills

ON A SUNNY Saturday afternoon, I'm watching my wife help our son learn to ride his bike. She runs a few yards with him, letting go to watch him swerve, slow down, wobble, swerve again, and fall over. They try a few more times, relying on the grass of a field in a local park to cushion his falls. At first he is tentative, and she shouts encouraging directions that are always a second too late. (*Turn the wheel left! Now right!*) Then suddenly he is off on a long ride, really doing it, shouting with joy. A moment later he falls. But now he's keen to practice and jumps up to try again. Somehow he has found the knack, coordinating the handlebars while pedaling, sensing and leaning and balancing as one set of fluid actions. He is mastering the task.

What does it mean to achieve mastery? Fundamentally, it means that we've learned to perform or do something well, without having to try too hard. Mastery requires knowing *what* to do, as well as *how* to do it. And when it comes to learning complex tasks, like swimming or playing a concerto (or negotiating!), the *what* and the *how* are different learning processes.

There are three keys to acquiring mastery: *preparation, process*, and *practice*. Preparation involves the moves we must learn to make as we approach a conflict. Process refers to the moves we make at the table, with the other side. And practice is the way we make these moves more like second nature. Let's take each one in turn.

PREPARATION

When we've got an upcoming negotiation or are facing a potential conflict, it's natural to find our thoughts and plans circling one another. Sometimes we try to escape the anxiety this creates by deciding to stop thinking and just "wing it" when the hour arrives. But while winging it is how we handle many social situations, it's a risky approach for conflicts and negotiations. Instead, we need to become more systematic in sizing up the situation.

Take a look at the negotiation process map in Figure 3 (on page 39). Having a process in mind helps us to do the right kind of preparation. It requires us to think about how we see the situation, and to think equally hard about how our counterparts see it. Having a process in mind leads us to consider possible questions to ask and possible solutions to offer. It encourages us to formulate arguments, and anticipate theirs. A preparation template like the one in Table 2 (on page 43) helps us do this. Although the list of concerns in Table 2 isn't exhaustive, a preparation checklist or protocol like this one reminds us to direct our attention toward certain kinds of problems or questions. Putting our thoughts into words – out loud or on a page – is the starting point for challenging ourselves and engaging others as we prepare. (For more tools you can use, see the Appendix or visit www.halmovius.com/resources.)

Preparing systematically steers our attention and creative energy toward the issues, options, packages, and arguments that

38

FIGURE 3

NEGOTIATION PROCESS MAP

→ → → → → → → → → → **RESOLVE** → → → → → → → → → → →

ESTABLISH	EXPLORE	INVENT	DECIDE	CAPTURE
A shared opportunity, problem or decision	Reactions to existing proposals	Options to create gains or bridge differences	Arguments (What makes this fair?)	Summarize what has been agreed
Key issues to discuss	Interests and priorities	Packages across issues	Closing trades, concessions	Define measures and milestones
Agenda: goals for meeting; timing; constraints	Areas of flexibility (If I...might you?)	Contingent commitments	In the event of an impasse: Do we walk away? Compromise? Bring in a third party?	Inform others affected by the decision
Who approves (or can veto) our outcome?	New issues (add, fractionate)			How can we do this better next time?

* LISTEN MORE THAN TALK *
* MONITOR TIME AND AGENDA *
* ACT WITH INTEGRITY *

might move the conversation in a productive direction. Preparing helps us manage the conversation, rather than simply react to what the other person says or does. Perhaps most importantly, it helps us to be proactive and to sidestep the anxiety and avoidance that the prospect of conflict so often brings.

PROCESS

Because negotiations can unfold so unpredictably, and in such varied circumstances, it's helpful to decide in advance how we intend to proceed, and why. The best way to do this is by following a negotiation process map. This is not the same thing as a meeting agenda, which is a list of topics or decisions with time allocated for each. Instead, a process map is an *explicit model* of the process we intend to follow in our conversation. It increases the likelihood that we'll cover the right things in the right order, and it gives us a way to orient ourselves in the moment if it seems that the conversation has gone off track. Figure 3 provides a process map you can start with and modify for your own use.

To understand what an ideal version of this process looks like, consider a brief negotiation between Lin-Sue and Craig. Lin-Sue is renovating her basement and has asked Craig to provide an estimate for completing the work. They sit down together not long after he sends an estimate.

	PROCESS/tactic
"I'm glad we can meet," Lin-Sue begins. "I'd like to have you do the work, but I need us to figure out a way to cut costs."	**ESTABLISH** Shared problem/ opportunity
"Okay," he says. "Then I think we should talk about the scope, timing, the fee, and cost of materials. I have an hour now, but can talk again later today if we don't finish."	Issues to discuss; agenda and constraints

	PROCESS/tactic
"If we can reach agreement, would you be able to commit to a work plan today, or do you need to consult with others?" she asks. "I can commit," he says.	Clarify approval process
"So I looked at your proposal, and I loved the design, but the materials and total cost look a bit high."	EXPLORE Reactions to existing proposal(s)

"The total project cost is important to you?" he asks.
   "Yes," she confirms, "that's the key, to be honest. I have a fixed budget."
   He nods. "What else is important?"
   She thinks. "I want to minimize the disruption."
	Interests and priorities

"I wonder, if we did the project in stages," he asks, "would it free up budget and be less disruptive?"	Areas of flexibility (if I . . . might you?)
"No, afraid not," she says, but then she suggests, "What if we used less expensive wood on the flooring – would that help reduce the cost for materials?"	New issues (add, fractionate)
He thinks. "Yes, that should help. And you know, if you were able to help with the painting, which is pretty easy, I could cut my fee." "Sure." Lin-Sue nods. "I can help with that. I used to paint houses."	INVENT Options to create gains or bridge differences
"So if you help paint," Craig continues, "and we use less expensive wood, then I can go down by about 20 percent. Or, we could go with the wood you liked, but that only reduces the cost by 10 percent."	Packages across issues
"If I could find the same flooring for a lower price, would that be acceptable?" Lin-Sue asks.	Contingent commitments
"Sure, I guess," he replies. "But I want you to know that I'm not charging you my standard mark-up on any materials."	DECIDE Arguments (what makes this fair?)

	PROCESS/tactic
"If I could pay you 50 percent now, in cash, could you reduce your fee by 5 percent?"	Trades and concessions

Craig looks down at his notes. "I'm not sure . . . I'd have to think about that. I'm already cutting it pretty close, and I could take other jobs."
  They both pause for a moment.
  "I can do that as long as you let me put our company sign on the front lawn while we're working."
  Lin-Sue exhales and smiles. "Sure, why not!"
	If impasse: Walk away? Compromise?

After a moment she says, "Can you and I just spend a few minutes now on a project plan? I'd like to figure out when the floor will be down and when I might have to deal with any interruptions to plumbing."	CAPTURE Record what has been agreed; Define measures, milestones
"Sure thing," Craig says, "and let me call my drywall guys and make sure they are free two weeks from now before I commit."	Inform other stakeholders
"Fine. And is there a best way for us to communicate going forward? Do you read texts? Emails? Or is it best to call?"	How can we do this better?

Of course, this is a simple and collaborative negotiation – an ideal. Most negotiations have more twists and turns, more complexity in the issues, and fewer cooperative and efficient moves by at least one of the parties. But we particularly want to have a plan in mind when the issues are complex and the other person is not cooperative. A plan gives a sense of direction and guides us toward action rather than reaction.

Bear in mind that a process map is meant to *guide* our strategy, not lock us mindlessly into a rigid sequence of tactics or behaviors. We might start a negotiation with friends by simply asking lots of questions about what they want, and why. On the other hand, a supplier bidding for a contract, or a lawyer in settlement chambers, has probably been required to propose a solution, and the

TABLE 2

NEGOTIATION PREPARATION TEMPLATE *

CONSEQUENCES OF NO AGREEMENT (CONA)	What happens to each side if there is no agreement? What alternatives do we each have? How attractive are they? What risks does each side face?
INTERESTS	What are our goals and concerns? Among them, which are most important?
QUESTIONS	What do we want to ask them? (For example: *What is important to you? Why? What else is important? Relative to issues A and B, and how important is issue C?*) What might they ask us? How will we respond?
ISSUES	What issues might be negotiable? How can we break down potentially troublesome issues into smaller ones, (i.e., fractionate them)?
PACKAGES	What packages of options (one option from each issue) are great for us and possibly good enough for them? How can we exploit differences in what matters most to each of us?
ASPIRATIONS AND LIMITS	What might we propose initially, that we could argue for with a straight face in view of our relationship goals? At what point (on one issue or a combination of issues) would the deal be less attractive than what we could get if we walked away?
ARGUMENTS	What arguments most effectively support our proposals *in view of their interests and* CONA? What benchmarks, standards, principles, or precedents might be most compelling to them? What arguments might they raise?
TRADES AND CONCESSIONS	What might we give? What will we ask for in return? How should each side's BATNA affect our flexibility? How should the time or opportunities to negotiate affect it?

---

* I sometimes use the plural *we* and *our* in these tools so that they can be used with teams or groups. When you use the tools for one-to-one conversations, simply replace the *we* and *our* with *I* and *my*.

conversation might begin with the other side responding to that proposal.

Core communication practices

A negotiation process map is only effective if we have the communication skills to guide the conversation forward. While there are specific steps under each of the five phases in our model, there are also key communication practices that span the entire encounter.

- **Listen more than you talk.** We imagine we spend more time listening than we actually do, and when we're nervous we talk far more than we plan to. Striving to listen will enrich our understanding of the situation and remind us to adopt a learning mindset during our conversations.
- **Monitor time and agenda.** Not every conflict can be resolved in the time available for a given interaction. If it looks like we're getting stuck on a particular step, or if we are going to run out of time, we need to decide whether to suggest another meeting, propose a scaled-down agenda, or offer to skip ahead to a concrete or final proposal to consider.
- **Act with integrity.** As my colleague Larry Susskind often suggests, it's wise to be "trustworthy, but not trusting." We don't have to resort to deception or coercion to get what we want, and as we'll see in Chapter 6, there are ways to deal with tough tactics from counterparts that don't require us to respond in ways that risk our reputation or demand we jettison our personal values.

Preparation helps us know what to say, ask, and propose. A good process suggests how and when we make those steps. Both preparation and process greatly improve our *potential* for a good outcome. But *practice* is the key. Practicing is what improves *performance*, making us more masterful when the time comes.

PRACTICE

Let me say at the outset: practicing a conversation aloud can feel ridiculous. You may fear that it will be artificial or strained, or worry that it's not really possible to simulate the negotiation with people who don't know the individuals or issues at hand. You may feel self-conscious and awkward practicing in the presence of other people, worrying that you'll be judged.

These are normal instincts. Everyone has them. But to develop mastery, we have to get over them. Practice frees us: once a particular set of skills is so deeply ingrained that we no longer need to grind our mental gears in order to execute them, we can move through the activity easily, leaving our conscious attention available for other challenging tasks, such as managing emotions or processing information. Based on years of experience coaching individuals and teams in all kinds of negotiations, I promise you that practice will help.

There are common negotiation process tactics that are particularly useful to rehearse. These include:

- Establishing or suggesting (concisely and clearly) the shared purpose, opportunity, or challenge
- Asking questions without sounding critical
- Responding to important or difficult questions
- Presenting and explaining the proposal (or preferred solution), and arguing for its merits
- Saying *no* clearly, and explaining why without sounding defensive

Of course, this is just a starting list. You should think about what might be hardest or most challenging for you, and make your own short list.

How should you practice? Sometimes we practice new tasks alone, sometimes with others. For negotiation and other complicated skills, coaching or feedback often helps. To master something complicated we typically need to take small steps, stringing together moves or actions until we finally ski down the mountain or play the song all the way through without error. Once we have the key moves down, we might even improvise and elaborate, pushing ourselves to try new and different approaches to the task.

Don't expect to get it right the first time. The more variations and approaches you try, the better the chances of finding convincing and effective words and phrases that sound like *you*, taking into account the relationship you have with the other person or group. My friend Dar Williams once put a sign up in her recording studio to encourage herself to write and finish a new group of songs: *Dare to Suck*. That is exactly the right attitude!

There are many ways to rehearse for a difficult conversation or negotiation. (I use the words *practice* and *rehearse* interchangeably.) How we do it will depend on the importance of the conversation, the time we have available, and the resources we can gather. In my own life, I've practiced having a brief conversation with a business partner while driving home from work alone. I've asked a friend to listen to the way I start what I know will be a hard conversation with a client. And I regularly run mock negotiations for corporate leaders prior to multimillion-dollar negotiations, sometimes with observers listening or watching (and sometimes with simultaneous translation from another language).

You don't need an audience to practice, or even a rehearsal partner. There is no reason you can't practice by yourself, even if it is just to rehearse for a negotiation with your in-laws or your landlord. Actors rehearse lines alone all the time, knowing that in the actual performance they may say things differently based on the choices the other actors make.

Rehearsing alone

Rehearsing alone is a minimal form of practice, but it is not a bad place to start when we don't have a trusted friend or colleague around. The famous Russian actor, director, and teacher Konstantin

46

Stanislavsky called units of action or dialogue *bits* (pronounced "beats") and rehearsed his actors by having them focus on one unit at a time. We can do something similar prior to a critical conversation by practicing a key move – our opening, for example – or by practicing responses to difficult questions or tactics our counterparts may use. (Note: You can leave a smartphone or laptop running, recording audio or video, if you think it will help. But don't do it if it will make you self-conscious, or otherwise block you from actually practicing.)

Everyone – *everyone* – feels weird rehearsing for a conversation. We have to expect that we will feel this way, just as we might expect that when we get up on the diving board, the water will suddenly look less inviting. Just start. Even if we are speaking the words out loud in an empty room, we will find that we sometimes come to a place where we have no idea what to say or how to say it. That's fine. Take a moment and brainstorm. Then try again.

Another way to rehearse alone is to practice a bit, then write down the key sentences that we think we will need. Then try saying them out loud again. Particularly when emotions are running high, writing words first can help us to find a place to start.

You might be shaking your head at this point. *"Does he really think it's reasonable to expect me to rehearse aloud for negotiations and difficult conversations?"* I really do, because I've seen over and over again how much it can help people be more relaxed and articulate. I've coached business leaders who faced the thorny task of selecting a new senior hire from among a number of internal candidates without alienating anyone. I've helped husbands and wives navigate the most important conversations of their marriages. I've coached teams preparing to negotiate with government ministries or powerful business partners. And I've taken coaching, from colleagues and friends. In challenging situations, practice is incredibly pragmatic and empowering. It helps us find the right words and phrases, the right opening lines, the right way to respond to criticisms or attacks, and the right way to propose solutions.

Rehearsing with a partner

When we are facing a difficult influence challenge or negotiation, it can help to find a trusted friend or colleague to help us role-play it. This person doesn't need to know that much of the backstory. We can spend two to three minutes explaining the issues and relationships, and describing the mannerisms and personality of the person we'll be facing. If we are rehearsing a response to a particular tactic or behavior, we can give our friend some lines to say. Remember, the key is not to perfectly simulate the situation; it is to get us to *practice*. As we'll see in Chapter 4, we are probably a lot less accurate than we think at predicting what the other person will actually say. That doesn't matter. The point is not to ready ourselves to spring a "canned" response on the other side when prompted, exactly as rehearsed. The point is to become more comfortable with what we sound like in the situation, and to try doing some things a little differently so that we're more effective in our communication, and more relaxed and efficient in our thinking, when the moment comes.

It's important to explain to our friend or colleague what we want to rehearse and *what we want in terms of feedback and advice*. It might be as specific and simple as "I want to make sure I sound clear." Or "I want to make sure I sound firm, but not angry." Or we might ask for more open-ended feedback: "I'd like your feedback about my approach, the way I'm communicating, and whether my questions and proposals are clear" or "I'd like to make sure my explanations and arguments are convincing." If we start by asking for more open-ended feedback, it is helpful to eventually ask for feedback on specific points. It's also important to ask for *encouragement*. Sometimes that is what we need most. As we'll discuss in greater depth in Chapter 5, a critical tool in bolstering emotional confidence is the feeling that others are with us and connected to us. So even if we want to hear about how we can improve, we should also ask our rehearsal partner to tell us what we're doing well. In fact, that is usually the best place to begin.

Running a group session

More and more companies and teams use some form of "mock" negotiations to help their people practice, and to better understand the challenges they face with counterparts. Larger sessions can be useful when we are entering the conflict as part of a team, or when we want to have feedback from more than one person.

Sometimes a consultant or outside expert can play the role of the regulator, attorney, or business counterpart across the table. Particularly when there are substantive technical, financial, or legal issues, seeking feedback from people who are familiar with the issues and situation can be helpful. But we can't assume that because they have expertise, and are playing the role of the other side, they will be able to tell us exactly what our actual counterpart will be thinking and feeling. Their guess is probably not much better than ours.

Mock negotiations work best when the participants are genuinely eager for help and are sheltered from excessive negative feedback or suggestions from too many observers. They also work better when our coach or colleague understands our process model. Even though practice is tactical in nature, we want those tactics to come from a solid and clear process strategy.

In larger groups, it is critical to limit suggestions about what to do differently. Poorly run mock negotiations consist of a practice session that runs for ten minutes, followed by 45 minutes of fifteen people critiquing the performance and suggesting twenty-three things to do differently. This is a recipe for disaster! Why? First, the negotiators will become defensive and/or demoralized. Second, no one can make multiple adjustments at the same time. Hearing ten to twelve ideas for what to say or do differently is overwhelming for anyone. A good facilitator or coach knows how to manage this process and choose the one or two suggestions that will be most useful or important to try.

Video or audio recording can be valuable here as well, particularly to note nonverbal behavior and team dynamics when teams are negotiating, rather than individuals. I ran a session a few years ago where a team of three technical experts practiced making a case to a regulatory agency. When they finished practicing their opening, I didn't say a word. I just played back the tape with the sound off. The whole team laughed out loud as they noticed how grim they looked, staring at the table or their own laps as their colleagues conducted their part of the brief presentation. No one watched anyone else speak, much less offered a supporting nod or smile during key points. "You don't look like you believe in your own proposal," I suggested gently. "You have to look like *you* believe in it if you want *them* to believe in it." They tried it again, and the difference was obvious.

The added benefits of rehearsing

One of the reasons it is so helpful to practice with others is that it raises the stakes, getting us out of our heads and into our voices and bodies. It also puts us into *action*, so we can discover that the phrases we worried about actually sounded great, or the phrases we felt sure about actually sounded unclear or unconvincing. Even five minutes practicing an opening or a pitch in a hallway with a colleague or friend can help us do it better!

A second reason to practice is that rehearsal exposes us to difficult emotions – our own, and the ones we imagine the other person might express. Just like with a phobic patient who is gradually exposed to something she fears, practice can help expose us to the behaviors and emotions our counterpart throws at us. It gives us a chance to become less reactive to them, and to plan and try out different tactics and words in response. When the time comes to deal with a difficult customer or neighbor or child, we're less likely to be derailed if we've practiced handling the emotions and behaviors that we're likely to encounter.

A third reason is that we may not realize how we come across. We think we are sounding authoritative, but we actually sound defensive or arrogant, for example. We think we are sounding respectful, but to others we appear uncertain or unforthcoming.

Finally, rehearsal can lead us to revise or refine perceptions, and identify gaps or assumptions in our analysis. Proposing something out loud often leads us to realize that we are actually not sure about the other person's interests, or our own information, or even our willingness to commit to certain options. It spurs us to think harder about how others might hear or see the situation, and to revisit or revise our awareness. I've run numerous mock negotiations where, in midstream, the negotiating team turned to their colleagues and asked, "Would we actually propose this? Or should we walk away?"

Developing negotiation mastery – the confidence to communicate effectively throughout a negotiation – relies on careful preparation, process, and practice. And these, in turn, begin with our perceptions. How are we doing? What does the other person want? What would we really walk away to? To be masterful at the table, we also need to develop greater confidence in how we *understand* the conflict situation.

As we'll see, this means expanding our awareness. Because as amazing as our brain is (and it is!), several decades of careful research show that we tend to take certain shortcuts and to see the world through a narrower lens when we're operating in the conflict crucible. To build mastery, we need to make sure we're planning and rehearsing for the challenge that truly exists, rather than an imagined one that we would prefer (or are most worried about). We need to see the challenge before us clearly, so that we think well and wisely about how to address it.

"Chance favors the prepared mind."

—LOUIS PASTEUR

CHAPTER 4

Awareness

Building confidence in our reasoning

IN GARRISON KEILLOR's mythical town of Lake Wobegon of *A Prairie Home Companion* fame, "all the women are strong, all the men are good-looking, and all the children are above average." This claim is funny not only because it can't be true (by definition, not all children can be above average) but also because it points to an instantly recognizable human foible. Research shows that we tend to enhance our rightness and goodness in our own minds, relative to other people around us – and we do so without even being aware of it.[1]

Think back to your last conflict. Who would you say was really at fault – you, or the other person? Perhaps, with the wisdom of hindsight, you'd admit that you both contributed to the situation. But in the heat of the moment, you undoubtedly felt certain that you were right and she was wrong. And she would have said the same about you. You know this intuitively: when it comes to conflict, there's always more than one side to the story.

Broadly speaking, there are three ways that our minds lead us astray: self-serving biases, the need for coherence, and egocentrism. I'll describe these in turn and then explain what we can do to try to achieve greater accuracy and clarity as we prepare to negotiate.

SELF-SERVING BIASES

Generally speaking, we all prefer to see ourselves as fair, competent, transparent, and virtuous. Psychologists call these flaws in our thinking *self-serving biases*, and while they make us feel better, they can also create or worsen conflict. For example, when researchers ask both members of a couple to estimate the percentage of household chores they do, their combined estimates typically total more than 100 percent.[2] If both partners believe they are doing most of the work, conflict is certainly more likely – if not inevitable. Other research has shown that:

- We rate ourselves as more objective than others,[3] and decide what is fair in ways that favor our own agendas.[4] (This is particularly true in the United States and other Western cultures.[5])
- We attribute our success to ability and skill, but our failures to bad luck.[6]
- In sports, we notice many more penalties or fouls committed by the rival team than by our own team,[7] and we see "media bias" that favors our opponents in stories about controversial topics.[8] Discouragingly, the more information we get, the more polarized we become, which is why political debates and feuds can continue for decades, with each side trumpeting their favorite facts and studies as "proof" that they were right all along.[9]
- We believe that things we own or invented are worth far more than others think they are worth.[10] For example, I

sometimes give out slightly fancy pens to half the participants in a workshop and ask them to jot down a minimum price for which they would sell the pen ($14 on average). I ask the other side of the room to say what they would be willing to pay ($4 on average). No wonder there is so much crap in people's attics and storage lockers: we're sure that Aunt Ethel's old oil painting is worth a lot – but it rarely is.

You may be nodding your head and thinking of how people you know are guilty of *all* of these tendencies. (But then, they are nodding their heads, thinking of you. You see how it works?)

It's no accident that we've evolved this way. This kind of optimism about ourselves and our prospects can be helpful to our survival, boosting mood, effort, and health.[11]

In conflicts, however, self-serving biases are not so helpful. Biased thinking can lead us to:

- Distort or misinterpret the problem or challenge
- Miss critical opportunities to get new and better information
- Overlook ideas that might leave both sides better off
- Make lousy arguments
- Throw good money after bad
- Needlessly act in ways that damage relationships

You can imagine how being convinced that we are right and she is wrong will pull us toward what I call the Fundamental Negotiation Error: trying only to influence the other person rather than recognizing that we can also problem-solve with them.

THE NEED FOR COHERENCE

A second problem is that we want the world to fit our existing views, and we want to believe that we can predict how things will unfold. Most of us are far more certain in our assumptions and assessments than we should be. Books like *How We Know What Isn't So, Thinking Fast and Slow, Negotiating Rationally,* and *Predictably Irrational* are excellent summaries of the variety of errors humans make when sizing up situations, other people, and themselves – and how costly these errors can be in negotiations and decision making. It's not that people are idiots (although some people . . . well, never mind). It's that we think in more than one way.

Systems 1 and 2

Can you hear the mental gears whirring? Right now your brain is perceiving and making sense of the words on this page, helping you breathe, monitoring background sounds in the next room or outdoors, and scanning sensations or signals that might take priority over continuing to read (for example, a sudden flash of light, a slight pain, a child's cry, or the smell of smoke). And your brain does all this, all the time, in the background of your awareness, for the most part without you noticing.

These tasks are handled every moment of every day by our *intuitive brain* – this is sometimes called System 1 thinking.[12] From the time we are babies, intuitive, automatic thinking helps us learn what is painful or dangerous, delicious or comforting, familiar or menacing. It lets us know that snakes and spiders are poisonous and helps us recognize the sound of mom's voice. From an early age we must learn to determine quickly whether other people are friends or foes, what they want from us, and how to relate to them. It's not surprising, then, that social judgments based on very brief encounters can often be remarkably accurate, even when we can't explain our reasons for them.[13]

Most of the time, intuition is our friend. It makes the world *coherent* to us. It prefers easy explanations to hard ones, and facts that affirm our existing beliefs over ones that don't. Its three favorite words are *that's so true*. Intuition has some major limitations, though. It is convinced by examples that come to mind easily. It seeks out evidence that confirms existing beliefs, and overlooks or downplays evidence to the contrary.

When we can't complete a task or make sense of something using System 1, we shift to System 2 thinking. System 2 engages in more careful searches for information, and more deliberate and cautious evaluation and planning. When we see an optical illusion, or something that doesn't make sense or that we've never seen before, our brain switches modes. It wants to know *what's going on?* Imagining the world from someone else's perspective; mapping out a secondary route in case of a traffic jam; doing math problems; moving through a safety checklist – this is System 2 in action.

However, using System 2 is energy-intensive, like running an air conditioner in a country where electricity costs a fortune. While our brain is only 2 percent of our body's weight, it uses 20 percent of our energy.[14] Because it burns so much fuel so fast, the brain can only run in System 2 mode for so long before it defaults to System 1 to save energy, returning to System 2 only when it has to.[15]

In conflict situations, intuition can lead us astray very quickly. In negotiations, it can cause us to give undue weight to the first number brought forward, which is why some negotiators resort to exaggerated first offers, and others start by quoting market rates or other benchmarks.[16] Our intuitive brain also assumes that specific numbers are more credible than round ones: for example, a contractor's bid of $1,012.75 feels more legitimate and less flexible than a bid of $1,000, which looks more like a ballpark estimate and therefore seems more open to negotiation. When we are in the conflict crucible, we need ways to access System 2 thinking so that we reach more careful conclusions about the situation before us.

EGOCENTRISM

While stopping to think more carefully about something can be useful, it doesn't guarantee that our perceptions and evaluations will be error free – particularly in social situations where the stakes are high. We are also at the mercy of egocentrism.

Egocentrism isn't the same as being egotistical or self-centered. Rather, it is the unconscious tendency to assume that other people will naturally see the world as we do. When we're in conflict with others, egocentrism leads us toward the following errors in thinking:

- **False consensus.** We overestimate how many other people believe the things we believe.[17] Surely everyone will agree that our neighborhood is the coolest one in town, or that this is a great song, or that a 5 percent cost-of-living increase is only fair. Right?
- **Fixed-pie bias.** More often than we should, we assume that if an issue is important to us, it will also be important to our counterparts, causing us to anticipate a bigger conflict than may actually exist.[18] We believe that the other side's motives will be directly opposed to our own. As a result, we assume that the "pie" is fixed – that their gain means our loss – and we conclude that tough-minded tactics will be the only way to get what we want (when, in fact, beneficial trade-offs may be possible).[19] Unfortunately, we are most prone to these kinds of erroneous assumptions when we are angry,[20] a common emotion during conflict.
- **Reactive devaluation.** We instinctively devalue suggestions or offers that come from the other side. We think, "If they're proposing it, it must be bad for us!"[21] (Of course, this is less likely when there is trust in our relationship.)
- **Fundamental Attribution Error.** We tend to explain other people's behavior in terms of their personalities, attitudes, or intentions, failing to adequately take into account the situational factors that contribute to someone's behavior. Think of it this way: when you're late for a dinner party, you know all the reasons – the directions were poor, traffic was terrible,

you had to stop and get gas, you got a phone call from an important client as you were departing. But when your friend arrives an hour late, smiling and apologizing, your brain associates the sight of him with the outcome at hand, forgetting to consider all the unseen situational factors that he experienced but you did not.

HOW FAULTY THINKING AFFECTS OUR CONFIDENCE

Clearly, our cognitive biases and limitations can make us *overly optimistic* about the merits and fairness of our own arguments, facts, stories, and proposals. And they can bias us toward events, stories, comparisons, and explanations that favor our version of things and our preferred outcomes. Once we have our story straight in our minds, our need for coherence causes us to latch on to the facts and arguments that we find most convincing, and to resist messages or evidence that call them into question. Being overly certain also leads us to prepare for a conversation in the wrong ways, or to assume that we don't need to prepare at all. "They're sure to see what a great deal we're giving them," we think.

But our limitations can also lead us to be *overly pessimistic* about what might be possible in a negotiation. When counterparts fail to see things the way we do, these same tendencies lead us to pessimistic conclusions. "My arguments are reasonable and reality-based," we think, "and theirs are inaccurate and possibly manipulative. I must be dealing with incompetent, unreasonable, or just plain dishonest people." More specifically:

- The **fixed-pie bias** leads us to assume that what matters most to us will matter most to them, and that what they want is in direct opposition to what we want. Consequently, we become less optimistic that a mutually satisfying deal is possible.

59

- **Reactive devaluation** causes us to anticipate that whatever they offer will be unfair or disadvantageous; we become less optimistic that their efforts or offers will be helpful.
- **False consensus** leads us to assume that others will see the situation in the same way we do. When we expect to have a hard time, we may assume that everyone else is also expecting a tough time; therefore, the exchange will be very difficult.
- The **Fundamental Attribution Error** makes us conclude that the other side's disappointing first offer reflects their overall attitudes and intentions (rather than constraints they may face – which we might be able to help them solve). This prevents us from exploring how they truly see the situation, and what might be most important to them, because we think we already know what they will say or do, telling ourselves, "That's just how they are."

Finally, egocentrism can lead us to *underestimate* our abilities as negotiators. Research has shown that if I ask you to perform some very simple tasks, which you can do easily, you will rate yourself as being quite good at those tasks relative to other people. But suppose I give you a difficult calculus problem, or ask you to juggle flaming sticks or ride a unicycle? Here the research suggests that you will rank yourself as *less* competent than other people. Why? We reflect on our incompetence at hard tasks and then rate ourselves as poor at them; egocentrism causes us to overlook the obvious fact that because the tasks are hard, others are probably also pretty bad at them.[22] This may be why so many of us not only dislike conflict but also feel we are bad at dealing with it. Conflict – the crucible of achieving material goals, building social capital, and managing emotions – is a difficult task. Small wonder, then, that we may believe we're poor at dealing with conflict: egocentrism inclines us toward an overly pessimistic conclusion about our abilities.

EXPANDING OUR AWARENESS

After hearing all this bad news, you might be feeling less confident in your judgment than ever. And you're not wrong to feel that way: research has shown that it's extremely difficult – perhaps impossible – to "debias" someone. However, there are things each of us can do to factor in these tendencies. It starts with expanding our awareness.

When we're approaching conflict or negotiations, it helps to widen our lens as we look at the situation and possible solutions. Whether we want to get someone to the negotiating table (through influence) or negotiate a mutually beneficial agreement once we're there, having greater awareness helps us to see more possibilities. Rather than convincing ourselves that we're right, zooming out like this helps us to ask questions and adopt a learning mindset. It can feel satisfying to villainize others – whether we're accurate or not – right up until we have to deal with the problem. At that moment, keeping an open mind is more helpful.

Building confidence in how we *think about* conflict is not about convincing ourselves that we are always right, or that the other person is wrong. *Rather, it means using techniques that help remind us that our intuitions may not be perfect.* This awareness can help us take a more deliberate approach to thinking about the situation and challenge at hand. The ability to see a problem more clearly, from different points of view, is like having a set of showroom mirrors that gives us the whole picture. It helps us to find and create more valuable agreements, more often, with less time and effort wasted. The research on this point is clear: looking at the problem through the other person's eyes will help us do better for ourselves.[23]

Why expanding awareness is hard

Research shows that negotiators who feel more certain about the accuracy of their beliefs end up being more satisfied than others about the deals they achieve, not because their results were better, but because they underestimated what was possible. "The pie was small," they think, "and I got most of it." [24] On the other end of the spectrum, after reaching an impasse, negotiators wrongly convince themselves that they were fighting a lost cause all along, and that no deal was ever possible. [25]

Similarly, we miss chances to learn by behaving in ways that elicit behaviors from the other side that confirm our initial views. [26] For example, we act aggressively or rigidly because we assume the other person will; they then respond to our aggression or rigidity with their own. These "self-fulfilling prophecies" cause us to confirm our initial assumption – that they are rigid and aggressive. We never discover that the interaction could have been different.

In other situations we learn from failure and from feedback. But in conflicts this feedback loop is highly unreliable. That's why adopting a more systematic approach to thinking about conflict is useful: it increases our chances of finding more valuable and useful outcomes.

Regardless of whether we are feeling confident or discouraged, bold or fearful, there are some best practices we should always use that encourage our brains to switch to System 2 thinking.

- **Get into their head.** Research shows that spending some time preparing for a conflict by thinking about the other person's point of view will help us find more valuable solutions once we are in the negotiations. [27] To generate better solutions, it isn't necessary to *empathize* with the other person's feelings (although this may help the relationship, or help soothe negative emotions). Rather, the key seems to lie in imagining how others see the situation – i.e., *taking their perspective*. What are their key issues? What matters most to them? What do they believe they would walk away to if there is no agreement? How do they think others will perceive them? Particularly when the situation looks bleak for us, it can be useful to think hard about what life really looks like for the other side if there is no agreement. It is all too easy to dwell on our own poor alternatives, and to forget that theirs may not be great, either.

- **Don't fear differences.** When it comes to building connections with others, we like to find common ground. Similar backgrounds, hobbies, experiences – these all build rapport and partiality in relationships. But remember that in negotiations it's helpful to look for different interests and preferences we can exploit through trades that give each of us more of what we value most.

- **Focus last on fairness.** In disputes and negotiations, we tend to fixate quickly on arguments about what a "fair" outcome should be. It's fine to do our homework on the going rate or other norms and precedents, and we should be prepared to back up our arguments with some facts and figures if we're asked to do so. But starting out by arguing whose numbers are more reasonable tends to devolve into positional arguments, risking an unnecessary impasse or inefficient split-the-baby compromises. It's more effective to hold off on arguing for our preferred options or solutions until we've first verified the other person's interests and assumptions. Only then can we know which compromises or solutions are likely to be more persuasive to *them*.

- **Stick to the plan.** In Chapter 3, I shared a negotiation process map for key moves we should make as we navigate through the conversation. Use it, and remember to stick to it in the moment. This is like having a map of a hiking trail rather than just "using our gut" to get through the forest: it orients us at each point along the way so we don't follow our intuitions down predictably unhelpful paths.

Checklists and reminders can help, too. As Atul Gawande argues in his book *The Checklist Manifesto*, checklists keep us focused on the right things when we're in complicated environments and faced with daunting or complex tasks. A good checklist directs our attention more systematically to the things that will help us make better plans and decisions. Checklists work well when they are short and when we know what they mean. I had one client who simply had two words written down: *Their* BATNA. It helped remind her that no matter how badly she wanted a sale, it always made sense to carefully explore how satisfied her counterparts were with their current solution, and to negotiate with that frame in mind rather than her own desperation.

Tempering excessive optimism

There's more than one way to be wrong-headed in a conflict. Unwarranted optimism and pessimism can both weaken our ability to negotiate a good outcome in our conflicts, and all of us will fall off one side of the log or the other from time to time. Whether we tend to feel overly optimistic or overly pessimistic depends in part on our own temperament (as we will see in Chapter 5), but it's also affected by circumstances, including the nature of the person we're in conflict with, and the relationship between us.

Research suggests that, on the whole, we are most likely to be overly *optimistic* in our beliefs and prospects in the following situations:

1. We believe we're in a better position to walk away if no agreement is reached.

2. We are in a position of greater power, such as formal authority, or we have the power to reward or punish the other person.

3. We're used to *feeling* powerful, perhaps because we're rich or politically powerful, or because we're used to getting what we want.

4. The issues we're resolving seem easy and familiar; we've dealt with similar issues in the past.

5. We expect the other person or side to be deferential and flexible.

6. Our relationship with the other person or side is not important to us – and maybe not to them.

7. We have a self-serving attribution style, tending to blame luck or circumstances for bad fortune, and crediting ourselves for success.

8. We're extroverts.[28]

It's hard to bring cocky people – ourselves included – back to earth. Research suggests that simply telling people how they might see conflict differently won't change their views, at least not right away.[29] Moreover, projecting certainty seems to generate social benefits: a "they-seem-to-know-what-they're-doing" effect. As psychologist Cameron Anderson and his colleagues have shown, even after the most overly certain people in a group have been shown to be no more accurate in their predictions than their colleagues, others in the group still rate them favorably.[30]

But excessive optimism can get in the way of useful preparation. If you're prone to optimism, or have someone on your side who is, try the following moves:

1. **Conduct a pre-mortem.** A "pre-mortem" analysis involves imagining that we have woken up at some point in the future and the worst outcome has come to pass.[31] Instead of capitulating to our demands, our tenant has filed a lawsuit; our sister isn't speaking to us; our employee has quit. The first step in a pre-mortem is to brainstorm all of the things that could have led to the bad outcome ("I didn't know what they wanted after all"; "They were angrier than I realized"; etc.). Once we have a list of hypothetical causes,

cluster them into themes (e.g., "I didn't understand their priorities" or "I behaved poorly"). Finally, think about steps we can take to reduce the risk of these factors coming into play. A pre-mortem focuses optimistic individuals on risk rather than reward, and can help balance perceptions and predictions.

2. **Consider the opposite.**[32] It is easy to argue a case we believe in. But the world's best debaters think hard about the strongest opposite case that could be made so that they are ready to address it if it arises. We are sure that our research into "the going rate" sets an indisputable benchmark for our contractor's fees. But what is the strongest case the contractor might make to the contrary? It helps to imagine these possibilities so that if or when they are raised, we don't react defensively and are able to provide a compelling and detailed set of reasons and arguments to support our claims.

3. **Recall a time when we were not so powerful.** Psychologists have found that getting people to write briefly about a time they felt powerless has a significant effect on feelings and outlook.[33] It might help to start a preparation session by reminding a cocksure colleague of a time when they (or the group) had less power, before moving on to analyze the current challenge using a System 2 mindset.

4. **Use a consultant.** Trusted or expert third parties can help check our rightness. Whether we bring in an outside counsel, a technical expert, or someone who has dealt with the other party in the past, a consultant can give our assumptions a reality check and suggest how we might improve our reasoning. For example, outside counsel in a lawsuit might know the judge well and help to identify weaknesses in our case. Getting a house appraised might help one spouse temper the other's certainties about what it will sell for.

Tempering excessive pessimism

However, there are times when we are unduly doubtful of our beliefs and underestimate our chances of negotiating successfully. This is most likely in the following situations:

1. We face terrible or highly uncertain consequences if no agreement is reached. In these situations, egocentrism may prevent us from considering the attractiveness or uncertainty of *the other person's* CONA, leading us to (unwisely) conclude that we should do whatever it takes to get a deal.

2. The other party has greater power, such as formal authority or the power to reward or punish us.

3. We're used to feeling helpless, perhaps because we've been poor or powerless in the past, or because we're used to having others get what they want at our expense.

4. The issues we're addressing are unfamiliar or complex, and therefore place great demands on the brain.

5. We've had a bad experience or outcome with this particular person in the past.[34] Under these conditions, we are trying to manage multiple goals (our own outcome, social capital, emotional or physical safety), so the task gets harder and our estimate of our abilities is further deflated.

6. We want to maintain a close or long-lasting relationship with the other person.

7. We are stuck in a pessimistic attribution style, attributing success to chance or other people, and failure to ourselves.

8. We are anxious – either by nature or in this particular situation. Anxiety causes us to narrow our focus and perception, losing track of larger opportunities and getting buried in details. When we feel insecure, anxious, or helpless about the prospects for a successful outcome, we often end up avoiding the conflict altogether or giving in too much or too quickly.

Four moves can help us shed our intuitive fears about a situation, empowering us to plan more proactively.

1. **Conduct a pre-rebus.** (*Rebus* is Latin for "success.") Imagine that we have worked hard and achieved a really good outcome ("She was interested in our proposal"; "He was not as angry as I had feared"; etc.). Once we've considered the factors that may have contributed to the good outcome, cluster them into themes (e.g., "I came in with several solutions and a willingness to listen" or "She was not as negative as I thought she would be"). Finally, think about steps we can take to increase the chance that these possibilities might come to pass. A pre-rebus analysis is good practice for pessimistic individuals because it focuses us on reward rather than risk, spurring us to act rather than fret.

2. **Remember that power comes from many sources.** If the other person or side has a much better fallback position than we do, or the power to reward or punish us, remember that there is also power in suggesting an elegant solution, demonstrating subject matter expertise, and being able to point to a strong precedent, example, or principle. We may have the power to affect the other person's reputation or future opportunities. We should never sell ourselves short just because our first thought or fear is that we need them more than they need us.

3. **Recall a time we were powerful.** Just spending five minutes remembering a time and place we felt powerful has been shown

to change mood and perceptions.[35] Doing this exercise can pull us out of a pessimistic state into one in which we begin to see more opportunities and feel less helpless.

4. **Seek support.** Time and conversation with an ally can bolster our spirits and help us escape our own pessimistic ruminations. Social support at moments of stress helps the brain think more clearly and creatively, and can help us identify leaps of logic or assumptions that are driven more by fear than by reality.

Of course, there's a lot more to be said about building confidence if we feel overly pessimistic in the face of conflict. Chapter 5 focuses on how we can cultivate the *emotional* component of confidence, which is hard to maintain when the heat is on and the stakes are high. But it can be done. Read on!

"Flowers are restful to look at. They have neither emotions nor conflicts."

—SIGMUND FREUD

CHAPTER 5

Poise

Building our emotional resources

QUICK – what's the opposite of confidence? The words that first come to mind are often emotional ones: *anxiety, panic, helplessness, doubt*. As we've already seen, confidence can be described as an ability, or in terms of mindset and awareness. But for many of us, confidence – or lack thereof – is more like a *feeling* than anything else.

It's true even for the pros. When researchers Kim Leary, Julianna Pillemer, and Michael Wheeler interviewed twenty seasoned negotiators, they found that all of them had "strong and conflicting feelings about negotiation" and that "even the optimists among them admitted feeling various degrees of anxiety about negotiation."[1] And as researchers Alison Wood Brooks and Maurice Schweitzer have found, anxiety leads negotiators to be more pessimistic about outcomes, set lower targets for themselves, respond faster to offers, and try to conclude negotiations more quickly (presumably to get them over with).[2]

Emotions can powerfully affect our ability to think and perform well under stress. It's tempting to view them as inconveniences or weaknesses to be overcome, but research suggests that we summon and maintain poise in stressful situations not by suppressing emotions, but by recognizing and managing them well.[3]

What's more, there is no getting away from emotion. Experience-sampling research has revealed that most of us (and men and women equally) are feeling at least one emotion about 90 percent of the time throughout the day.[4] And that's not a bad thing. True, some feelings are unpleasant; none of us loves feeling bitter, anxious, envious, resentful, enraged, disgusted, empty, or heartbroken. But emotions are also intrinsically rewarding. Whether you rate yourself as a highly emotional person or more even-keeled, you'd probably agree that a life devoid of love, lust, joy, pride, awe, satisfaction, interest, surprise, and curiosity would be dull, at best.

Emotions are prevalent in our lives because they have at least two critical functions. First, they help us interpret our experiences and make better decisions.[5] Is this person friendly or hostile? Does this activity feel fruitful or useless? Am I in danger? Should I relax now, or work harder?

Second, emotions help us to bond deeply with others, to feel hopeful or satisfied, to look forward to experiences, and to appreciate other people and their experiences and ideas. Both positive and negative emotions are essential to our survival.

But emotions are also taxing, and we run into trouble when we don't know how to harness or cope with them. When it comes to conflict, there are several ways our emotions can prevent us from acting masterfully and exercising good judgment. They can:

- Cause us to frame situations as hopeless,
  which leads us to avoidance
- Blind us to opportunities or ideas
- Inhibit us from thinking creatively

- Drive us to lash out in ways that damage relationships
- Make us behave in ways that violate our own values
- Cause us to miss opportunities to negotiate
  and problem-solve with others

And that is the *short* list.

NEGOTIATION IS COSTLY TO
OUR SOCIAL BRAINS

My friend and colleague Jim Coan, who is a social neuroscientist, once startled me by suggesting that negotiation is a "very unusual social interaction." I asked him to clarify what he meant, since it seemed to me that negotiations are commonplace. "I don't think negotiating is something the human brain was really designed to do," he explained. "For most of human history we lived in small groups, where disagreements were probably rare and most of us shared a whole set of common goals. That's the situation our brains are literally born expecting. Because negotiating can put a relationship at risk, it feels hard and unnatural. This is why humans have created institutions and rituals to handle conflict. Only recently have societies become so complex that each of us needs to negotiate so often."

In recent decades, research by social neuroscientists has produced enormous insights about the social nature of our brain's organization, and the importance of relationships in regulating our own feelings. Humans are social animals, and scientists are learning how our brain and nervous system have been shaped by our social tendencies and social ecology.[6] Negotiating is disproportionately stressful because conflict is a roller coaster of possible cooperation on the one hand, and possible competition or treachery on the other.[7]

Small wonder, then, that navigating through conflict can feel like wandering through an emotional minefield: we're trying to get what we want from others who might potentially help or hinder us, while regulating our emotions and dealing with theirs. The conflict crucible is so fiery precisely because our brains are designed to be exquisitely attuned to "friend or foe" signals from others. Every negotiation creates a different crucible. How will we define and measure success? What kind of relationship do we hope to cultivate? What do they want from us, and how costly would it be for us to give it to them? Will they think less of us if we push hard, or if we are pushovers? What kinds of emotions are we most vulnerable to? There is a great deal to be gained and lost in every exchange, much of which is perceived and managed beneath the surface of the interaction. It's no wonder most of us find that the struggle to maintain our emotional equilibrium – our *poise* – is the greatest challenge to our confidence in the midst of conflict. (Recall that among all the daily stressors we experience, the most stressful by far is interpersonal conflict.[8])

THREE COMMON TRIGGERS
OF EMOTION DURING CONFLICT

Other people's behavior in a conflict – or, more accurately, *our perceptions* of their behavior – can trigger a variety of powerful emotions, and our ability to anticipate the emotions and maintain our poise in those moments can mean the difference between achieving a good outcome and deepening a relationship, or walking away frustrated, perhaps having burned bridges.

In situations involving conflict or potential conflict, there are three common triggers of emotion:

- We perceive lack of progress toward our **goals**.[9]
- We perceive violations of **fairness**.
- We perceive violations of **relationship expectations**.

Notice that in each case, we are *perceiving* something. As we monitor other people's behavior, it is wise to make friends with these little phrases:

"It seems that . . ."
"It sounds as if . . ."
"It feels like . . ."

This language (even if it remains in our heads, unspoken) reminds us that we are always *interpreting* what other people are doing or saying. We're comparing what we see and hear to our assumptions and beliefs about what should happen, what they should feel or believe, or how they should behave. Are the other people helping us achieve our goals or hindering us? Are they treating us fairly? Are they acting in a way that scares or reassures us? That values or demeans us? It's useful to remember that our emotions during negotiations don't just happen; they come from what we're hearing, seeing, and thinking.

Goal frustration

As we see progress toward agreement or resolution, we may feel positive emotions such as excitement, hope, satisfaction, joy, pride, or relief. But if we perceive that the possibility of agreement is fading or slowing, then frustration, anger, disappointment, or worry may bubble up instead. In the first few minutes of a negotiation, we may feel great hope as our counterparts talk about their desire to find common ground with us. But as things slow down or hit a snag, we may begin to feel worried or irritated. If we perceive progress on some fronts but not others, we'll feel a mix of emotions, which can be confusing. And when we're not sure whether we're gaining ground or losing it – when our proposed solution is apparently ignored, for example – feeling anxious is also a natural consequence.

Fairness violations

Humans (and other primates) have a deeply ingrained sense of fairness. Fairness is always based on a comparison, either to a standard we have in mind, or the outcome someone else got. Another person's seemingly unfair suggestions or version of events can trigger very strong feelings, from anger or envy to sadness and resentment or anxiety.

An even more powerful set of emotions can arise if we perceive that a *process* is unfair. In fact, researchers find that most of us are willing to live with a decision we don't like if we feel the process by which it was reached was fundamentally fair.[10] This is partly why mediation and other forms of assisted negotiation can be so beneficial: aside from helping people create better deals, a good mediator can also implement a process that feels safer and fairer to participants.

Relationship expectations

Relationship expectations refer to how we expect to be treated. When we're in conflict with people who are close to us, or on whom we rely, perceived violations of relationship expectations can trigger intense emotion, as we'll see in Chapter 7. But even when we're negotiating with someone we'll never see again, or someone whose relationship with us is not important, we still hold expectations about how people in this kind of situation ought to deal with one another. For example, a customer may believe that it is always appropriate for a seller to treat the customer with respect. Or two colleagues may have different ideas about what it means to handle a workplace disagreement in a "professional" way.

Sometimes we perceive a mismatch between the substance of a message and the way it is delivered. In the workplace, for example, many of us default to emailing or texting critical feedback or complaints that would be better handled face to face. Of course, we do this to manage our own anxiety, but the mismatch between the importance of the message and the impersonality of the medium can come across as disrespectful or autocratic. A public example of this occurred when popular head coach Lovie Smith was fired from the Tampa Bay Buccaneers by telephone, and fellow coaches around the NFL expressed dismay.

Relationship expectations are powerfully influenced by social norms – these three in particular:

- **Status-related.** Whether or not we are aware of it, we all hold beliefs about the nature of our connection to various people, and how they should communicate with us. Violations of relationship expectations often involve status or power. We become angry when other people talk down to us, or imply that they are more experienced or knowledgeable or insightful than we are. We become suddenly enraged or embarrassed when a child "talks back" to us, or when someone speaks to us in a way that doesn't acknowledge our status. We become irritated or nervous when someone who barely knows us addresses us intimately.

- **Cultural.** Cultures differ in their communication and behavioral norms, and acting or communicating in ways that inadvertently violate cultural expectations can also be potential triggers. In cultures that value harmony, for example, outwardly expressing anger or disgust to a stranger might be unthinkable, whereas in cultures that value self-expression, people tend to be more direct in expressing what they feel. The first time I went to Rome, I turned a corner to see two men fighting over a parking space, yelling at one another, gesturing wildly, their faces only inches apart. I had just arrived in the country after spending a month in Japan and Thailand, and the contrast was shocking; I thought perhaps they would kill each other. But they didn't. In fact, they yelled a while longer and then simply walked off. In Italy, unlike Japan, positive and negative emotions are expressed easily and openly, even among strangers. Similarly, I discovered when I moved to California in the 1980s that the humorous rants that seemed to bond people in New England were off-putting to my new friends, who responded by suggesting I might try yoga or kite-surfing. Positive emotion was considered a good way to connect, but negative emotion was . . . totally uncool, dude.

- **Physical.** The most extreme violation of relationship expectations occurs when other people make us feel awkward, unsafe, or threatened. They may do this by speaking too loudly or aggressively, moving toward us, being too physically familiar, or making an implicit or veiled threat ("I would hate to have to . . ."). Perceived violations of physical norms trigger emotional arousal, and lots of it. Our heart rate quickens, stress hormones like cortisol and testosterone get released and fire up our brain's limbic system – the older, emotional part of our brain that prepares fight-or-flight strategies. To counter this, we can name what is bothering us ("You're getting loud now, and it's scaring me"), take action (step away, suggest taking a break), or change the subject. If we value the relationship, we should find a time later to provide feedback directly or indirectly (through a colleague, for example) to the other person in the form of a request.

In general, withdrawing from situations where we feel persistently or dangerously threatened is the best plan, because our brains won't be good for much problem solving until we feel calmer and safer. In close relationships it may be possible for the other person to change gear ("Okay, I'm sorry") and to offer reassurance or soothing that permits problem solving to resume.

Others' actions can trigger us by blocking our goals, breaching our sense of fairness, or violating our expectations about how they should speak to us. But it's also important to understand *environmental* sources of emotion, which can make us more or less easily disturbed by what others say and do.

HOW ENVIRONMENT AFFECTS MOOD

If triggers are the match that lights the fire, mood is the kindling. While some of us tend to be more anxious or crabby than others, everyone has better and worse *moods*. People in better moods tend to be more cooperative, more generous, and more creative.[11] Moods affect our perceptions, judgments, and behaviors most *when we're unaware of them*.[12] It's therefore wise to try to create conditions that are more likely to put us and our counterparts in a better mood, if we can, and to at least be aware of the effects of environmental conditions if we can't control them.

Social psychologists have had a lot of fun manipulating subjects' moods without their awareness. Turns out there are several ways we can change someone's mood by changing environmental conditions.

Environmental factors

1. **Odor.** Yes, it's true. Even subliminal levels of good and bad odors can affect perceptions, judgments, and performance. Bad smells cause people to like things and other people less, and to be less creative and less generous. Good smells produce better mood, better problem solving, more ambitious goal setting, higher self-efficacy, and more generosity. In one study, subjects who negotiated in pleasantly scented rooms set higher goals, made more concessions, and were more likely to want to be collaborative in the future.[13]

2. **Time of day.** Although people differ in how they feel at various times of day, research suggests that most people feel best in the middle of the day.[14]

3. **Noise.** Uncontrollable background noise turns out to be a great way to worsen anyone's mood and make them less likely to cooperate with others.[15]

4. **Weather.** People report being happier with their lives overall if asked on a sunny day, as opposed to a rainy one. [16]

Of course, we can't always control these things – but that may not matter as much as we might think. Research suggests that when we are simply *aware* of these factors, we subconsciously take them into account, which can reduce their effects. For example, when researchers Norbert Schwarz and Jerry Clore asked study subjects about current weather conditions *before* asking for a rating of life satisfaction, the weather ceased to have an impact on overall life satisfaction. People mentally noted that it was a crappy day, and adjusted their evaluation to take this into account.

It makes sense to scan the room as we enter into a negotiation; if unavoidable irritants are present, we can acknowledge them to ourselves, and perhaps name them to others in the room if it seems appropriate to do so. When we have little control over the situation or setting, just being aware of these factors can reduce their emotional effect.

Physiological factors

Psychologists and neuroscientists have found that mood can also be shifted by several physiological factors.

1. **Food.** If we have to have a difficult conversation, it's best to do it on a full stomach – and even better to try to ensure our counterpart has eaten recently, too. Not only does hunger have a major effect on mood, it has also been shown to have a direct effect on tangible outcomes in negotiated conflicts. Management professor Shai Danziger and his colleagues found that parole judges in Israel began the day by granting requests 65 percent of the time. That percentage dropped throughout the morning, however, hitting zero right before lunch (no parole requests granted). After lunch, parole approvals went back up to 65 percent again! The same pattern repeated in the afternoon: after a break, the rate of granting

parole went from zero back up to two-thirds. These patterns held steady even after controlling for the severity of the crime and many other factors. This came as a total shock to the judges themselves, who believed that there were no differences in how they administered the law during different times of day.[17] The theory is that having a full stomach, which activates our parasympathetic (calming) nervous system, may translate into more generous and cooperative judgment and behavior.

2. **Stimulants.** Caffeine has been shown to elevate mood during stressful tasks.[18] But if we have a high level of baseline stress, we may not want to consume too much caffeine, as it can also worsen anxiety by revving up our heart rate.

3. **Sleep.** As any parent knows, not getting enough sleep makes us more prone to irritability. It also makes us more anxious, less able to learn and remember information, and less creative.[19] My colleague Jessica Payne at the University of Notre Dame is a leading sleep researcher who coaches leaders and teams in optimal performance. Simple interventions she prescribes have led to major improvements in decision making. For example, one team now no longer makes key decisions at the end of meetings; instead, they wait until the next morning. The same holds true for conflict: when we are tired, we are less likely to be able to learn and to see new ideas and options. We are less resilient and find it harder to regulate our own emotional state. If it is not possible to reschedule a negotiation when we are exhausted, we must be aware that we are likely to be more pessimistic and judgmental than may be warranted.

4. **Pain.** Chronic pain has been shown to cause anxiety, irritability, and depression, but there is a complex relationship between mood and pain. Being in a worse mood actually seems to worsen pain.[20] If we have an injury or condition causing pain, it is a good idea to

do two things: 1) make ourselves as comfortable as we can before negotiating, and 2) take into account the fact that we are in pain as we move through the conversation. For example, if our pain levels are high, we may ask to delay making any key decisions during the meeting, or could choose to set up a series of short meetings rather than one long one.

5. **Posture.** Management professors Dana Carney and Amy Cuddy have found that adopting an expansive "power pose" before a challenging task can raise testosterone and increase our appetite for risk.[21] This is exemplified by the classic Superman pose or victory pose – arms akimbo or outstretched, feet planted wide apart on the ground.[22]

6. **Facial expression.** Sometimes we may be able to improve our mood just by smiling. In one study, researchers had subjects hold a pencil in their teeth in a way that simulated a smile. These subjects found a set of cartoons funnier than a control group did. Simply asking people to produce emotional expressions has a similar effect on mood.[23] Smiling or laughing in a stressful situation may improve your mood. (You may want to step out of the room, though, to avoid confusing the other side! Or crack a good joke.)

7. **Exercise.** Interestingly, exercise can be a mixed bag for negotiators. Researchers Ashley Brown and Jared Curhan found that people who dislike negotiating feel worse and achieve worse outcomes if they negotiate while they are exercising rather than while they are sitting still. But *more confident* negotiators do better and feel better when they walk or exercise during the negotiation. The reason? When we dread negotiating, our brain interprets our physiological arousal as anxiety. When we feel optimistic, the arousal is interpreted as "excitement" that spurs us on to more successful actions and tactics.[24] If we are already feeling bullish about an upcoming encounter, taking a brisk stroll in advance of our

meeting might pep us up further. But if we feel anxious, keeping our heart rate low is probably a better way to prepare.

Just as checklists can be useful for cultivating more deliberate mental habits, we can use a *body and environment scan* to remind ourselves of factors that might affect our current state – and we can take action if necessary to bolster our mood. We will be better grounded emotionally if we've made allowances for the conditions we're operating under. We might even print out Table 3 and glance at it from time to time to remain aware of our emotional state and what might be causing it (aside from what we're seeing and hearing from a counterpart).

TABLE 3

FACTORS AFFECTING OUR MOOD

ENVIRONMENTAL	PHYSIOLOGICAL
• Odor	• Food
• Time of Day	• Stimulants
• Noise	• Sleep
• Weather	• Pain
	• Posture
	• Facial Expression
	• Exercise

We've covered three common triggers of emotion when we're in conflict situations. We've covered environmental and physiological factors that can produce better or worse mood states (which predict better or worse problem solving and cooperation).

There's one final and important source of emotion in conflicts and negotiations, though:

You.

KNOW HOW YOU GO

Individuals differ emotionally in four key areas:

- Temperament
- Levels of emotional awareness
- Meta-emotional tendencies
- Coping strategies

As you read about these areas below, think about where you fit in. In Chapter 9, we'll discuss some tools and techniques you can use to identify your own tendencies and develop and adapt your practice to take them into account.

Temperament

For decades, theories about personality were hamstrung by poor and incomplete – if very popular – measurement tools and ideas. But in the last 25 years, empirical research on human personality has converged around a dominant theory and model, with thousands of studies and measures providing fairly consistent patterns of results across more than fifty countries.

This model, sometimes called the Five Factor Model or "Big Five" personality theory, comprises five major personality factors or traits: *neuroticism* (negative emotionality), *extraversion, openness to experience, agreeableness,* and *conscientiousness.* Note that some of the factor names have a nuanced meaning beyond their popular definition, *Extraversion,* for example, means positive emotionality or sociability, not just a tendency to be outgoing. (To take a free test and find out your overall personality, go to www.halmovius .com/resources.)

Each of the five traits has six "facets" or subscales (although some measurement tools vary a little bit at these lower levels). Genes account for roughly half of our major trait scores,[25] and variations in these traits have been found to correspond to variations in the size of specific brain structures.[26] By the time we are in our late twenties, most of us are fairly set in terms of our personalities across the five major traits, although extraordinary events or changes in circumstance can produce significant shifts. As we move from young adulthood to old age, we get a bit less negative, a bit nicer, and a bit less open to new things.

Interestingly, the tendency to experience negative emotions (neuroticism) and positive emotions (extraversion) are uncorrelated. We can be high on one and low on the other, low on both, or high on both,[27] and our self-reported tendencies largely match what close friends see in us.[28] Similarly, humans differ in how intensely we feel emotions. Some of us go through life without many dramatic peaks and valleys, while others feel emotions deeply.[29] These differences are detectable in early childhood and tend to persist throughout life for most of us.[30]

For both positive and negative emotionality, most people are in the middle of the pack, but some of us are very high or very low. If you score high in the tendency to feel negative emotions (more easily anxious, depressed, irritable, self-conscious, hopeless, impulsive), take a bow. Why? Those of us higher in *neuroticism* (and I am one) excel at detecting threats, taking protective actions, and/or alerting others. We are the twitchy gazelles in the herd, more vigilant than the others. Being anxious is taxing for the individual but benefits the group by helping protect it in potentially dangerous situations.[31]

People high in *extraversion*, however, are more sensitive to rewards and are better at pursuing them. Extraverts actually do worse in zero-sum haggling situations; they are more likely to fixate on other people's first offers, and make concessions more quickly than non-extraverts, perhaps because they want to feel the reward of reaching agreement (whatever its quality).

Those of us high in *agreeableness*, with a tendency to be trusting, compassionate, and polite in our dealings with others, also do worse in zero-sum negotiations. We are naturally affiliative and put other people first. (Think of Ned Flanders, the unflappable nice-guy neighbor from *The Simpsons*.)

There is something freeing about discovering and embracing our own biologically rooted tendencies. In more individualistic cultures, humans spend incredible amounts of money and energy on trying to feel happier. While evidence suggests that there are ways to do that (get enough sleep; maintain healthy relationships; practice gratitude),[32] it is probably also wise to understand our underlying tendencies so that we make plans and act in ways that account for our tendencies, rather than fighting them.

Our traits, and our temperament in particular, tilt us in certain directions as we think about situations, weigh whether to enter into or avoid them, and decide how to act within them. If we are more anxious generally, we are likely to be extremely anxious when it comes to working up the nerve to confront someone about a problematic behavior, and we may find it harder to approach negotiations feeling calm and focused. That's just how we go.

But it doesn't mean that we can't develop confidence, or get great results! Basketball legend Bill Russell reportedly got so nervous before games that he regularly got sick; he was still one of the greatest ever to play the game. Many actors and musicians report having terrible performance anxiety, but they are still fantastically successful. Even CEOs of major firms vary enormously in their self-reported levels of anxiety.[33]

Managing temperament

For those of us high in negative emotionality, it is wise to recognize and accept this. We may become anxious or discouraged more easily than other people, and stay in that zone longer. Luckily, however, there are things we can do to pull ourselves up.

1. **Reinterpret feelings.** We may find it helpful to reappraise or reinterpret our feelings – view anxiety as excitement, for example, or see our anger as passion for a good process or a fair result.

Similarly, we can reframe or reappraise the situation – viewing it as an opportunity rather than a fight; as a chance to learn rather than persuade; as a challenge rather than a sign of trouble. Allison Wood Brooks at Harvard Business School has shown that simply reinterpreting anxiety as excitement (using self-talk like "I'm excited!" or "Get excited!") can help people perform a subsequent stressful task with greater confidence.[34] Reinterpreting nervousness or dread as par for the course, rather than a sign of doom, can be a powerful move as we prepare for and carry out negotiations.

2. **Recruit allies.** Whether we just need someone to listen to our problems, or whether we'd like someone to help us brainstorm or even come with us to a meeting, the physical presence of another person (even someone we don't know well) has a remarkable effect on the brain, calming down those parts of it that are associated with pain and distress.[35] We will think more clearly, feel better, and possibly get a good idea or two if we have someone listen to our situation, ask questions, suggest ideas, and offer consolation or support. When we have a conflict or problem with someone, we may keep it to ourselves for many reasons: embarrassment or defensiveness, anxiety, reluctance to burden others, or belief that no one could really understand the situation or person we're dealing with. But these are distortions. It is almost always helpful to talk conflicts through with a trusted advisor or friend. As someone who has coached a wide range of people and teams over two decades, I can say with some certainty that managing conflicts and relationships is a *normal* source of anxiety for almost everyone, and a *normal* issue to seek help with – whether from a professional or a friend.[36]

3. **Be your own ally.** Sports psychologists have found that having athletes use positive self-talk ("I can do this") improves performance[37] – and self-talk that uses the second person ("You can do this") may be even more effective.[38] Psychologists studying

non-athletes have found the same thing. Some subjects talked silently to themselves using "you" or their own names while preparing to give a speech, while others used "I" or "me" while preparing. On average, people in the former group ended up feeling calmer and more confident than those in the latter, and gave talks that were judged to be better by the audience. It seems that getting a little distance from ourselves by using "You can do this" helps us better regulate our emotions by taking us "outside" ourselves.

If we rate low in negative emotionality, we may feel less stress and inner turbulence than other people during conflicts. However, we may also be more likely to underprepare in advance of negotiations, since positive emotion leads people to use less intensive mental and analytical processing.[39] We could balance this by finding someone who is more prone to anxiety and therefore more likely to push us to think systematically in advance, rather than "winging it." By the same token, remember that our less energetic and optimistic colleagues are not necessarily lacking in their enthusiasm for our ideas or their trust in us. They may be more focused than we are on anticipating and preparing for a disappointing result. When we feel frustrated by their apparent anxiety or pessimism, we can calm ourselves by remembering that their emotional behavior at a given moment may have more to do with what's going on inside them than with what we are doing. And we can thank them for their commitment to making sure there are no nasty surprises for us. Similarly, it's helpful to remember that the person we're dealing with across the table may experience the situation as far more threatening than we do, and may need to take things more slowly or deliberately.

Emotional awareness

People differ in how easily and elaborately they can name what they are feeling. Some people are virtual maestros of emotional awareness, accessing their feelings with ease, and often describing nuanced blends of feelings ("I'm happy that Tony's team won; sad that we lost; a little jealous, I guess. Also worried that we won't be asked back next year.") Women are, on average, better than men at describing what they and others are feeling, and this holds true even taking variances in verbal intelligence into account.[40] (Sorry, guys.)

Being more emotionally aware can be helpful in conflicts. It means we can tell the other person how we are feeling, or monitor our own feelings with greater accuracy, and we can select coping tactics more deliberately, rather than just impulsively acting or reacting. However, this awareness increases the likelihood we will get stuck in our feelings, ruminating or analyzing emotions to death rather than acting to solve the problem or situation that might be causing them. If you are highly emotionally aware, remember that while this "fine instrument" can be an advantage, it can also hamstring you if focusing on emotions gets in the way of action.

Managing emotional awareness

Those of us higher in emotional awareness must remember that other people may not be capable of this. We may be surprised at how many people are unable to name emotions; they might say "I feel bad" or "I feel like hitting something."[41] They may find our ability and willingness to talk about emotions off-putting.

Remember also that our fluency may lead us to default to emotion-focused coping skills, such as talking about feelings. It is important that we balance these with problem-focused coping techniques, and in particular that we use preparation tools to focus on concrete ideas, proposals, and actions that can help resolve the issues.

For those of us lower in emotional awareness, who find it harder to access and name what we are feeling, try using an emotions checklist, like the one in Tool 7 (on page 186).

Meta-emotional tendencies

The term *meta-emotion* was originally coined to describe how parents respond to the expression of emotion in their kids.[42] Essentially, it means "feelings about feelings," and it refers to how, when we experience an emotion or witness others expressing it, we may become conditioned – by family, peer groups, or broader cultural norms – to have a particular reaction to it. These conditioned responses often happen unconsciously, but they can have a major effect on how we experience and express emotions in the midst of a conflict.

We might feel ashamed of our anger, for example, or worried about expressing pride, or guilty about feeling attracted to someone. These reactions can happen so quickly and unconsciously that we sometimes bypass the first emotion on our way to the second. For example, we are disappointed and saddened when we are turned down for a date, but we find that sadness curdles immediately into anger.

Our meta-emotional style or conditioning is important because it links back to the conflict crucible. Some of us are highly distressed when we encounter negative feelings in ourselves or others. These responses are emotion-specific, giving every individual a complex and precise blend that can be just as hard to understand in ourselves as it is to decode in others. We may not feel comfortable talking about our fears, but have no problem talking about our anger (or vice versa). Our feelings about feelings can make it hard for us to identify what we're feeling, or may create layers of emotion we have to deal with, directing our attention and energy away from problem solving in the negotiation.

If we are going to manage meta-emotional tendencies, the first step is to become more aware of our temperament *and* our feelings about specific feelings. Then we can think about whether it would be useful to reframe certain emotions when we feel them. ("Hey, there's my trusty old anxiety again, looking out for me" is a more productive response than "Oh crap, I'm feeling shaky!")

What about our feelings about the *other* person's feelings? Here things get more complicated. Witnessing emotional outbursts in others can trigger a host of assumptions, fears, and impulses, which may or may not be based in reality, and may not be helpful in resolving the problem at hand. A toddler's screams might elicit panic from one adult, concern and coaching from another, disapproving reproach from a third, and disregard from a fourth. (Parenting tip: concern and coaching makes for healthier, smarter kids.[43])

Our feelings about other people's feelings are specific to the person and situation. If our relationship with a counterpart doesn't matter to us at all, their disappointment in our proposal, for example, may not have much of an impact. However, if we deeply value the relationship, their negative response will be more concerning.

Power dynamics also matter: researchers find that negotiators who feel powerful relative to their counterpart are less concerned about the other person's feelings, while those who feel less powerful pay closer attention to the other person's feelings and take them more seriously.[44]

(Bear in mind, though, that there are many different kinds of power, including the power that stems from meeting another person's emotional needs. When a close relationship is at stake, even the most powerful magnate, tycoon, politician, or monarch may feel vulnerable, or act deferentially. Ronald Reagan, former president of the United States, was said to depend enormously on his wife, Nancy, and to defer to her in important decisions. As leader of the free world, he had greater formal authority than she did, but he depended on her emotionally, which gave her power in their relationship.[45])

Coping strategies

Finally, people differ in how they cope with difficult emotions under stress. Some of us tend to favor strategies that focus on self-soothing; others focus more on problem solving.

- **Problem-focused coping strategies** include analyzing, organizing, gathering information, and planning; seeking advice or support; and reframing the problem.[46]
- **Emotion-focused coping strategies** include distraction (doing other things), seeking pleasure (in food, drink, drugs, or exercise), calming ourselves down (meditation, prayer, progressive relaxation, or breathing exercises), venting to a friend, and journaling.[47]

These strategies are all designed to help us manage emotions, but they don't deal with whatever may be causing the emotions. Both types of coping strategies have their place. Research shows that when we can't change a situation (for example, if a friend has died, or if we're stuck on a long boat ride), self-soothing is most helpful. But if we *can* do something about a situation, problem-focused strategies are generally a better choice. In fact, frequent use of problem-focused coping is correlated with lower stress levels and more stable and positive moods.[48] When it comes to conflicts and negotiations, therefore, we have what might be called the *coping strategy paradox*:

> If we expect the conflict or negotiation to be a lost cause, we rely on soothing our own emotions; however, this can lead us away from the problem-focused coping techniques that would increase the chances of negotiating successfully.

Gender and coping strategies

Women experience negative emotions more frequently and intensely than men do;[49] they report experiencing more stress, both daily and over time (perhaps because in most cultures they have, on average, less socioeconomic power than men). Women and men also differ in sources of stress. Women report experiencing stress more often around health and relationship issues, whereas men more often report stressors relating to finances and work.[50] Women also report using emotion-focused coping strategies more often than men. Researchers find that men are more likely than women to drink or use other substances to help escape unpleasant emotions, while women are more likely than men to worry and ruminate, dwelling on and analyzing emotions.[51]

In general, women are more physiologically reactive to interpersonal conflict than men, showing greater increases in cortisol, for example (a stress hormone).[52] This may reflect an increased emphasis on preserving social capital and managing negative emotion – a gender difference in how conflict crucibles are constructed and experienced.[53]

Diversifying our coping strategies

If you're not sure which coping strategy you tend to favor, use the Coping Styles Quiz, Tool 9 in the Appendix, to help you understand your tendencies better. And be aware that at certain times it may be helpful to deliberately cultivate a different approach from the one you naturally default to.

Bear in mind that if we are going into a negotiation with an expectation that a bad outcome is inevitable, we will probably resort to emotion-focused strategies (to calm ourselves or escape from the situation). While these are useful skills to have in the toolbox, we will likely find that problem-focused strategies are more powerful over time because they help remove or reduce the *source* of stress.

If we find ourselves leaning toward self-soothing strategies when a problem-focused approach might be more productive, we can remind ourselves to consciously follow the steps in the negotiation process map (Figure 3) outlined in Chapter 3. We will feel better about any influence challenge or negotiation if we have a systematic way to prepare for negotiations, and a set of key process moves in mind. This means taking the other person's or side's perspective, discerning the interests that lie underneath positions, and taking steps to improve our BATNA if no agreement is reached.

Build negotiation mastery by preparing for the encounter with a plan in mind, and by rehearsing key moves out loud with a trusted friend or partner.

Another problem-focused move that can help put us on a firmer emotional footing is to commit to disciplined curiosity. Thinking about all of the arguments we have to win, or brilliant ideas that we need to create, can quickly become overwhelming. Instead, ask questions like:

- What do I want to learn?
- What does the other person really want?
- Why are they acting this way?
- How do they see me?
- Why am I so nervous?
- What's most important to me?

Thinking of the conflict as a mystery to be solved, as opposed to a battle to be won, is a good way to take some pressure off.

However, those of us who prefer logic and analysis, and who like to "get right down to the problem," may benefit from a reminder to take stock of our state, mood, and physical needs before, during, and after a tense negotiation. Why? Because ignoring emotions and mood does not make them go away. Instead, feelings that have been ignored or suppressed often leak out in unhelpful ways in the heat of the moment, influencing (and limiting) our awareness, and hampering our ability to make masterful moves.

PUTTING CONFIDENCE TO THE TEST

In the next three chapters we'll focus on special challenges in negotiations. In Chapter 6, I'll equip you to deal with difficult people and tactics. If you've ever been up against people who use explosive displays of emotion, throw their weight around, or resort to tough tactics, you'll know how hard it can be to negotiate productively with them.

Equally challenging for very different reasons are the people closest to us, who often seem to possess supernatural abilities to rile us up or shut us down. Chapter 7 focuses on how to negotiate more confidently and effectively in close relationships.

In Chapter 8, I'll explain how negotiating on behalf of others can add a layer of challenges, as we deal not only with counterparts across the table but also our own group or team. Negotiating on behalf of others requires additional moves to help you maintain mastery, awareness, and poise.

"We don't devote enough scientific research to finding a cure for jerks."

—BILL WATTERSON

CHAPTER 6

Foes

Dealing with tough tactics

JERRY'S MORNING commute is not going well. He's about to enter the most important meeting of his young career, and it feels like a long, slow pull into the Death Star.

Last week he received a letter from Caitlyn, his client's purchasing manager, demanding a 25 percent cut in the fees charged by Jerry's firm and threatening to "take the business elsewhere" if necessary.

Arriving at the meeting room, Jerry takes one last sip of coffee, squares his shoulders, and knocks on the door. The client's negotiating team sits across the table. They don't stand when he enters.

"Sorry I'm late," he says, as if reporting for sentencing. As he meets Caitlyn's gaze, he feels his face flush and his heart start to pound.

He tries to open positively. "We're glad to be working with you on the extension. We can't trim fees by 25 percent without changing the scope of work. But I'm ready to explore how we can do that."

Caitlyn rolls her eyes and then leans forward, eyebrows arched. Speaking slowly, as though to an imbecile, she says, "This is very disappointing, Jerry. We're not here to *explore*. We're not here to *adjust the work*. Either you are going to come into line with market rates, or we're going to have to pull the business and give it to someone else. Your services are over-priced. The market has moved. You're not competitive anymore."

Jerry counters, managing a smile, "Well, I think we actually are very competitive, when you look at – "

"Jerry. Jerry." Caitlyn holds up her hand. She has a bored look on her face, but her voice and eyebrows are raised. "Please. I'm not here to listen to excuses. I have to do what's best for our business." Talking over his attempt to interject, she continues, "I think we're done here." She stands up and walks briskly toward the door, followed by her two colleagues.

"I'll give you to the end of the day," she calls over her shoulder.

As the door closes, Jerry's mind goes blank. His heart is racing. He tries to summon calm, exhaling and sitting up in the chair. Caitlyn represents his biggest client, and the choice seems to be lose that client or make a concession that means the work becomes unprofitable. Either outcome will be a huge blow to his career.

Now what?

DEALING WITH formidable opponents can be among the most anxiety- and stress-provoking experiences we will have in life. It's not just that our goals conflict with theirs. It's not just that they have different ideas about what's fair or reasonable. As we try to achieve our material goals while managing emotions and protecting rapport, they proceed as if there were only one possible result: getting what they want.

That may or may not be true; they may in fact be using emotions *strategically*, and expressing attitudes they don't really feel, in order to influence us. But their behavior, tone, language, and facial expressions convey an unmistakable impression: "My goals matter; yours don't. I don't care about getting along with you. And your feelings are *your* problem." No wonder we get knocked off our game plan. They're making the Fundamental Negotiation Error, and they seem to be getting away with it.

MASTERY WHEN DEALING WITH TOUGH TACTICS

Sticking to the negotiation process map outlined in Figure 3 is more challenging – but even more important – when dealing with an opponent who slings tough tactics at us. Remember that mastery involves creating a mental habit of thinking *systematically* about the components of a situation in ways that we can discuss with others. We still need to uncover underlying interests and issues, create packages and arguments, and analyze what we'll walk away to if no agreement is reached. And we need to do all this while resisting our opponent's attempts to steamroll over us and wrest control of the conversation.

Caitlyn may *behave* as though the relationship is unimportant, or threaten to walk away, but Jerry should spend time thinking carefully about where his company would find itself if Caitlyn pulled the business – and where Caitlyn's company might be. Even if Jerry is desperate to keep the business, he may be overlooking how difficult life could be for Caitlyn's stakeholders if they have to find a new service provider.

The goal in taking a little time to analyze the situation is to get our brain to move from reacting intuitively – and emotionally – to thinking systematically about the situation, from our own point of view and through the other person's eyes. *Getting to Yes* implores us to "separate the people from the problem,"[1] and in situations where we are facing difficult people, that is an excellent (if quite difficult) first step. It still leaves us trying to solve the problem, however, perhaps without any help from them. For that we need a mental map setting out how to proceed.

There's an old saying, sometimes misattributed to Sun Tzu: *Strategy without tactics is the slowest route to victory. Tactics without strategy is the noise before defeat.* The point is, we need both strategy and tactics – but a big-picture process map is indispensable. A map in our hands will help us decode what the other person's tactics are trying to accomplish, and when we might be straying from a more productive process.

The map in Figure 3 is a starting point, but my recommendation is that you take to heart the basic sequence (Establish, Explore, Invent, Decide, Capture) and use your own words to define the tactics that are most relevant for the situation you face and the time you have. It can be as simple as 1-2-3 (frame the problem, explore options, decide) or far more complicated, as in highly complex technology or policy negotiations, where problems may need to be taken apart before they are put back together again. The clearer we are about how we will proceed, the clearer we will be about how our counterpart's actions are derailing the *process*, rather than harming the relationship. Focusing on the process, rather than our own emotions, is powerful armor.

Focusing on process also suggests that we will often need to spend time at the outset *negotiating how we negotiate.* Jerry made a mistake by diving right in with a response to Caitlyn's demand ("We can't trim fees by 25 percent without changing the scope of work.") A more powerful move would be to say, "Okay, well, I'm glad we can sit down today. I'm aware of your demand that we cut fees substantially. What I'd like to do now is learn a little more about what is driving that, then explore what might be possible, and then give you several proposals that might work for both of us." Let's imagine how that might play out:

CAITLYN: We can do that, Jerry, but I'm here to tell you that you're going to reduce your fees by 25 percent or we're walking out that door.

JERRY: You certainly have to do what's best for your team. But help me understand where 25 percent comes from. Why 25? What's the goal here?

Notice that Jerry isn't saying no here, or apologizing, or pleading. He is shaping the process and getting more information. But he can only do that if he has an idea of what a good process should look like, and what his goals in that process should be.

Similarly, when we set the agenda for a meeting, it is often useful to quickly spell out how we would like to proceed. When they say, "You'll have to come down on price," or something far worse, we can say, "Okay, sounds like price is important. But let's spend a minute just discussing how we're going to proceed. I'd like to learn more about your goals and concerns, and explain ours."

Responding to tough tactics

- **Invoke the relationship.** When a person or group speaks or acts as if our relationship is unimportant, but we suspect otherwise, a disarming communication move is to *name the relationship we want* as part of the shared problem. For example, after they've opened by criticizing our proposal, making a veiled threat to walk out, we might say, "I'm glad we could meet today; I guess we need to figure out how to cut costs while still giving you great service and protecting our good relationship."

  Or in a dispute closer to home we might say, "Thanks for coming over. We want to find a way that you can practice the drums while keeping the peace on our side of the fence. It's important to us that we stay good neighbors." If they openly proclaim that they don't care a bit about any future relationship, we'll need to make a judgment as to whether that is true and adjust our approach accordingly. Sometimes we need to simplify the crucible by abandoning our attempts to preserve a relationship that isn't worth fighting for. Why should we work on three problems while they only work on one?

- **Formulate your version of no.** It's useful to think about what your version of "no" sounds like. How we walk away from a situation can mean the difference between reengaging later or burning bridges entirely. One recipe I really like is Bill Ury's Yes–No–Yes formula,[2] which in the case of negotiation might sound something like this:

    YES: I really want to make sure we come away today with a great outcome.

    NO: I can't agree to what you are proposing . . .

    YES: . . . but I am willing to work hard to try to find ways to give you what you need while ensuring I can live with the outcome.

- **Counter their claiming tactics.** Foes are not going to let us off the hook. They will surprise us with new tactics and frustrate us with their tried and true ones. Tough claiming tactics are used as influence tools; when a foe uses one it means she wants to convince us that she is right and we are wrong, or that we have no choice but to agree. There are commonly used "tough tactics" in negotiation, and it helps if we can name, anticipate, and rehearse for them. Table 4 suggests how to recognize and respond to four common claiming tactics.

TABLE 4

FOUR COMMON CLAIMING TACTICS
AND HOW TO HANDLE THEM

CLAIMING TACTIC	WHAT IT SOUNDS LIKE	WAYS TO HANDLE IT
Extreme opening offer	"I can only do one day a week; you'll have to cover on the other six."	**INQUIRE:** "Help me understand why you can only do one day." "What makes that fair?" **COUNTER WITH AN EQUALLY EXAGGERATED OFFER:** "I was actually counting on you covering six days. So clearly we'll need to figure something out." **SUGGEST A DIFFERENT PROCESS:** "Hmm. We're far apart on what's possible, it seems. But help me understand what you're dealing with right now, and perhaps we can think of some workable options."
Positions or demands	"I can't take less than $5,000 for the project."	**REFRAME/INQUIRE IN TERMS OF INTERESTS:** "You have a budget constraint – is that right?" "Why $5,000? Where does that come from?"
Anchoring (throwing out a number)	"The going rate is $15 an hour; that is more than fair."	**PUT THEIR ANCHOR IN CONTEXT:** "A rate of $15 per hour may be fair for some kinds of work, but for more experienced labor I believe the rate is closer to $20. On such short notice I've had colleagues actually charge $25 to $30 an hour." **DISAGREE AND REFOCUS:** "I don't agree with your assessment, but before we talk about what's fair, can we spend a little more time on the big picture and what is important to you? Is the pay rate the most important issue we need to deal with today?"

FOUR COMMON CLAIMING TACTICS
AND HOW TO HANDLE THEM

CLAIMING TACTIC	WHAT IT SOUNDS LIKE	WAYS TO HANDLE IT
Ultimatum	"Take it or leave it."	**ANALYZE (IN ADVANCE):** What is their CONA? Would they really walk away? What is our CONA? Are their terms worse or better? **REFRAME IMPASSE AS AN OPTION:** "Either of us can walk away, but that could be costly and risky for both of us." **GET THEM TO *MAYBE*:** "I'm not sure I can say yes to that. Help me understand why you are asking for these terms. What makes them fair? How do they meet your interests and ours?" **IGNORE IT:** "Let's talk about what you want today and see whether we can think of ways to get it for you."

Finding the words

Of course, it's helpful to rehearse our responses. After we've thought about what our foes' versions of these tactics will sound like, it's a good idea to have someone say them to us so we can practice responding. Even if we end up hearing something different in the actual encounter, and/or saying something different from what we prepared, the fact that we practiced will help us remain calm. A little voice in our head will say something like, *I knew this was going to happen. No big deal. Here goes.*

When we are dealing with someone who is intimidating or obnoxious, likely to use tough tactics, or just more powerful than we are in a given situation, rehearsal is a way to do our own *exposure therapy*. Exposure therapy helps people get over their fears by exposing them, gradually, to more and more realistic and comprehensive versions of what they fear (from looking at a picture of a snake, for example, right up to handling one).

In the context of conflict, the first step is to think about the words we fear our opponents will say, and the way they will say them. What words or emotions will trigger us? Infuriate us? Fill us with anxiety? Think about the conflict crucible: What is at stake for us? How much does the relationship matter? What are our most important interests? Which emotions are most troubling – whether in us or when expressed by our foes?

Remember, too, that in negotiations, negative emotions are most commonly triggered by:

- Goal frustration
- Fairness violations
- Relationship expectations

In our work with clients – even those who are seasoned business negotiators – my colleagues and I have found that writing down the things we most dread hearing from the other side provides a strong starting point for rehearsal. Writing down possible threats, criticisms, and demands makes the job of preparing more tangible and manageable.

Writing down possible triggers, or talking them through with an ally, is just a first step. We need to practice a little, too. The words we think about saying often come out very differently when we actually say them. If we are able to recruit help, we can get our friend or colleague to play the role of the other person and say the things we think will be most irritating or unnerving. Just exposing ourselves to those actions or statements makes them less ominous and more solvable – particularly if our ally can help us think of responses.

One of the most challenging aspects of dealing with tough tactics is that they can quickly constrict our thinking. It's not easy to slow down and use open, inquisitive System 2 thinking when our System 1 instincts tell us we're being backed into a corner. But it's essential. Curiosity can save us from becoming defensive, or reacting in other ways that prevent problem solving. And taking time to evaluate our options carefully and deliberately will save us from panicking and making a bad decision based on the unpleasantness of a momentary emotion.

AWARENESS WHEN DEALING
WITH TOUGH TACTICS

Let's come back to Caitlyn for a moment. Why do some people negotiate like jerks, pushing hard for what they want in ways that seem to cut off connection and spark negative emotion? There are a number of possibilities. Here are nine:

1. She is an unpleasant person – possibly a sociopath – who treats everyone this way.

2. She really has it in for Jerry and wants to put him in his place.

3. She believes that effective negotiation requires making demands and threats.

4. In this situation, she feels powerful because Jerry's company is desperate to keep the business, and other companies have already yielded to similar threats.

5. As a purchasing director, she is only rewarded for getting a significant rate reduction, and she really wants a bonus for hitting her targets.

6. She heard that Jerry was going to raise rates significantly and has opened with a demand for rate cuts as a counter-anchoring strategy.

7. She is under tremendous pressure to cut costs; failure to cut costs will mean she is out of a job.

8. She is in a terrible mood because of something else that has happened, or because of mental or physical pain.

9. She is trying to impress someone on her team who has suggested that she has been too easy on Jerry in the past.

Of course, Caitlyn's real reasons for behaving as she does could be some combination of these, or none of them. The truth is: we don't know. We don't know why she is being such a jerk. We don't know whether she is going to follow through on her threat to pull the business or not. We don't know whether she really has to have a 25 percent cut or is just opening with that demand and hoping to eventually achieve 10 percent.

But if you're like most people, you probably find explanations 1 or 2 most convincing. She seems like a jerk. When people act aggressively or emotionally toward us, their behavior is the most salient thing we see. Falling prey to the Fundamental Attribution Error leads us intuitively to think, *What a jerk!*

That is System 1 working. We need to maintain awareness in moments of tension, and that means cultivating disciplined curiosity. In my experience, the following are the three most likely reasons that Caitlyn is acting as she is:

1. **Mindset: She believes this is how one negotiates effectively.**
Caitlyn might have a very competitive notion of what it means to
negotiate. Maybe her mentor or boss did it this way, or she picked
it up from books, courses, or films. If we begin with the notion that
people are simply doing what is familiar, rather than doing something to be intimidating or destructive, their behavior becomes
less threatening.

2. **Incentives: She is driven by narrow or specific incentives
set by her organization.** Sometimes organizations measure and
reward negotiators for achieving very narrow goals, such as closing
a sale (no matter how poor or overpromised) or cutting spending
(no matter the longer-term consequences or risks to the health of
the organization).[3] We might call this the *mismeasurement problem* in negotiation. Our short-term interests ("I've got to get a
discount") can eclipse our bigger-picture priorities ("We need to
become more profitable or we'll be in trouble as a company"). Even
in our personal relationships it's easy to become so focused on winning the little battles that we end up getting far less in the end.

3. **Power: She sees herself as having more power than Jerry.**
People may feel powerful for a variety of reasons: seniority, formal authority, control over desired resources, a good BATNA. On
average, men are more competitive and assertive than women, but
both men and women become more assertive as they rise in organizations.[4] Psychologist Paul Piff and his colleagues have shown
that the wealthier among us are actually less charitable, trusting,
and helpful in their behaviors than people who have less money,[5]
while Adam Galinsky and his colleagues have shown that inducing people to simply *feel* powerful causes them to behave as if they
care less about what others think and feel.[6] Feeling powerful, in
short, emboldens us.

It's easy to leap to conclusions about other people's character deficiencies or secret intentions. Like a matador sidestepping an onrushing bull, it is helpful to step away from our own quick thinking. Disciplined curiosity, the curiosity and systematic awareness that we force ourselves to adopt, is the way to do this. It may not change their behavior, but it will put us in a more empowered frame of mind, make us less prone to knee-jerk reactions, and – most importantly – give us time.

POISE WHEN DEALING WITH TOUGH TACTICS

Sometimes the *way* others address us rattles us far more than the words they use. Like dry brush, emotions sometimes ignite while our brain is still processing the information. When someone expresses negative emotion toward us, our physiology typically begins to activate even before we're aware of it (and guys, we're more extreme here). In Chapter 5, we identified some key moves you can use to summon and maintain poise.

But what about *the other person's* emotional behaviors? How should we respond when someone is right up in our face, or coolly threatening to do things that will make us worse off? What should we do when someone insults us, or treats us as if we're idiots? It is hard to plan in advance for these situations, because expressed emotion is contextual; it can mean different things depending on who is saying it, and when. For example, anger expressed by a powerful person toward a weaker one has a much greater effect than anger expressed by the weaker person. A child's rage may be less threatening to a parent than the converse, and the boss's fury at a subordinate's action will cause more fear than the subordinate's anger. Researchers have found that negotiators who express anger at an offer will achieve greater concessions only if their anger is judged to be real; otherwise it is ignored.[7]

The first step toward handling difficult emotions in others is to increase our level of emotional awareness. Emotional behaviors have specific social functions, and it helps to be able to understand and name them.

Anger

Expressed anger signals a violation of boundaries.[8] It accompanies messages like, "Stop it!" and "That's mine!" and "Don't do that again!" The ability to express anger in a close relationship can be a good thing; it means that one or both people are signaling to the other that something was said or done that was not okay. (In fact, the frequency of expressed anger in a relationship predicts absolutely nothing about how happy a couple will be years later, or whether they'll still be together.[9]) Nevertheless, anger can be very unsettling to some of us, particularly when expressed by a stranger or by someone who is more physically powerful than us or who controls resources we care about. When someone expresses anger toward us, we should respond with the following key steps:

1. **Take steps to ensure we feel safe.** Monitor our heart rate and level of fear; ask the other person to step back or calm down; or take a break from the conversation. We can also invite other people (a colleague, a therapist, a coach) into the situation to help set ground rules and manage the conversation.

2. **Acknowledge.** Stop whatever is happening in the conversation and acknowledge or inquire about what we are seeing or hearing. ("I can see you are angry about this.")

3. **Separate the emotion from the problem.** It is important to separate the emotion from the legitimacy of our proposal or the process we want to follow. Some people get angry in conflicts when they start to believe that they will not get what they want. That doesn't mean we should give it to them.

4. Test whether the anger is genuine or simply strategic. Old-school negotiators often pretend to be angry in the hope that it will pressure the other side to make concessions. Naming what we are seeing and then asking questions about why the person is so angry can help root out real concerns, or determine whether it was just a strategic display.

Criticism and disparagement

Criticism (along with its more destructive cousin, contempt) suggests that in some way *we* are defective or blameworthy. It can take the form of "you always/you never" statements, and is distinct from complaint, which is about expressing displeasure with another person's *behavior or actions*. Saying "I wish you had parked the car closer to our house!" is a complaint. Saying "It's so like you to park a block away" – even with a smile and a perky tone of voice – is a criticism. Criticism can also involve what John Gottman and Jim Coan call "negative mind reading" (e.g., "You didn't really care about my show" or "You didn't even want to come, did you?"). Disparagement is criticism of an entire group ("That's so typical of them").

Criticism is common but highly corrosive. In fact, frequent use of criticism by spouses is one of four predictors of future divorce. It is almost always followed by one of two responses: defensiveness or countercriticism. Defensiveness ("That's not true!" or "I did not!" or other responses delivered in a whiny tone) encourages more criticism, and we end up in a cycle of attack/defend that gets us off a problem-solving path. Countercriticism ("Maybe so, but you always leave the lights on") also escalates and maintains conflict, derailing us from the problems at hand and causing us to focus on one another's perceived deficiencies.

What can we do instead?

- **Don't take the bait.** Recognize the criticism/complaint distinction and the criticism/defensiveness trap. Like many old patterns, we may have to blunder into the trap many times, even after we know about it, before we start to get better at interrupting the pattern. When we recognize that we are in a criticism/defensiveness spiral, we might suggest that we take a break, or we could ask the other person or team to describe what they want, rather than what they don't like.

- **Name and reframe.** When we hear people say "You always" or "You never," or hear them make the problem about us rather than our actions or ideas, we must ask them to be specific. Tell them we hear that our action/idea/proposal is objectionable, but suggest that nothing is to be gained by making it personal. (People who are being critical sometimes don't realize that they've made it personal and may backtrack once we point that out.) We can reframe "always" or "never" criticisms in terms of the problem that a future agreement needs to address. Saying, "We need a way to make sure that doesn't happen" will carry the conversation away from defensiveness and toward problem solving.

Contempt

When criticism is present, expressions of contempt are sometimes not far behind.[10] Contempt, an emotional mixture of anger and disgust, is more damaging to relationships than criticism. It communicates a lack of respect and can take the form of sarcasm, mockery, eye-rolling, and insults. Its function is to belittle, hurt, or humiliate by diminishing the other person. Because contempt is so personal and so hurtful, it can be extremely difficult to stay cool, but doing so is a very powerful move. Try the following techniques:

- **Reframe contempt as skepticism.** We can disarm the other person by reframing their contempt as a sign of skepticism. This deflects the emotion they are expressing to the problem or matter at hand, rather than to us. For example: "You seem to have some skepticism about the rates I've quoted. Why is that?"

- **Ask for a complaint.** We can also try saying something like, "You seem to have a really strong reaction to what I'm suggesting. Are there specific ideas or options here that you are most concerned about?" By getting the other person to name what is troublesome, we might be able to shift the discussion toward complaining (focusing on the problem rather than on us). A specific complaint can be addressed as part of a shared problem or opportunity.

Domineering

Domineering is an attempt to control the situation by forcing others to agree with our ideas, opinions, requests, or statements. Donald Trump is an almost nonstop exemplar of domineering. The most common nonverbal signs are body leaning forward, chin down and eyebrows raised (picture a gloating Jack Nicholson), finger pointing or jabbing, and head cocked to one side. When Caitlyn raised her hand, said "Jerry. Jerry," and talked over him, that was domineering. Domineering behaviors include:

- **Incessant speech:** Talking without breaks, and talking even louder when someone attempts to interrupt
- **Invalidation:** Making someone wrong ("You don't know what you're talking about")
- **Lecturing:** Citing authorities, or appealing to an ambiguous "everyone" ("Everyone agrees with me on this")
- **Low-balling:** Asking questions with predetermined answers ("We shouldn't have to pay for your mistakes, right?")

The good news is that while domineering sounds terrible, and most people find it truly irritating, Gottman's research suggests that it is not as destructive to relationships as criticism or contempt. To manage domineering behaviors, we can try the following four moves:

- **Reframe their behavior** in our head as a defensive maneuver that is designed to control the situation. Even though it is irritating, we can defuse the behavior simply by thinking, *Wow, this person is the domineering champ!* We will feel calmer and more patient.
- **Signal.** Sometimes raising a hand or gesturing that we have something to say will carve out a little airtime.
- **Ask for the floor.** When they have finally finished speaking, or have indicated that we can respond, we can thank them for their comments and (knowing they will try to interrupt) ask permission to have the floor for the next two minutes – or however long we think we will need.
- **Express anger.** We can sometimes stop domineering behavior by interjecting with a simple "Stop!" or "Enough! Can I speak now?" Remember that anger signals a boundary violation of some kind. If we express anger briefly and with conviction, it can sometimes dislodge our foe from this strategy.

It helps to have allies in the room when someone is domineering. We can make eye contact with our allies to help calm each other down, and when we ask for the floor or express anger, the others can validate this response. It's easier to regain control of a situation when others are there to help.

Disappointment

You can't please everyone all of the time, and when other people express disappointment in us, it can make us feel guilty that we've let them down, or anxious that agreement is not within reach. Depending on our relationship with them and how strongly they react, we may find their disappointment almost unbearable, especially when we are by nature a people pleaser, and may feel a strong urge to make a concession of some sort.

Like anger, disappointment is often feigned by hard bargainers, as in the so-called flinch, which is an attempt to provoke an immediate concession. Even if the person's disappointment is genuine, reining in our impulses will allow us to recalibrate our own emotions and respond intentionally. Rather than rushing to mollify the other person, it can be helpful to learn two new habits:

- **Commit to silence.** Sometimes the best thing to do if we are worried the other side won't like our proposal – or if our counterpart has a habit of guilt-tripping us – is to lash ourselves to the mast as Odysseus did. In this case, it means remaining quiet for ten seconds after they respond, leaving them room to elaborate or explain. This will prevent us from rushing in to soothe them by apologizing or making a concession. Disappointment can instead be a prelude to renewed problem solving.
- **Acknowledge and inquire.** Respond to their disappointment with questions asking for information rather than an apology or concession: "Okay. Why is that disappointing? Where does it fall short, exactly?" We might learn something new about what they value, or we might find that they have no coherent answer, in which case we've called their bluff.

Threats

Like an ultimatum, threats can be used tactically to try to influence the other side through coercion. In negotiations, they often signal an intention to walk away unless terms are met. "This is our last offer; take it or leave it." We can respond to threats just as we would to an ultimatum, based on our analysis of the situation and where we are in the process. But there is one caveat.

Personal threats, along the lines of "I will hurt you," are obviously more emotionally toxic than tactical ones, particularly when they are made by someone more powerful, and are delivered with expressions of anger or contempt. In such situations it is usually best to name the tactic and end the conversation; then change the communication or negotiation process, bringing in outside help or hiring an agent or lawyer. Our response might sound like: "You're threatening me, and I'm not going to continue this conversation now. When we do continue we'll need a better process."

And please note: we should respond this way *even when we are more physically powerful than the other person.* Personal threats often lead to escalation, and "They said something that bothered me" is not a good excuse in court or anywhere else. The same goes for ultimata that contain personal threats ("Bring the money tomorrow or you will be in a world of pain"). This is not negotiation; it is simply intimidation, an influence tactic that implies your safety is at stake. The best thing to do is stop, go get help, and avoid escalation in the moment.

KEEPING YOUR COOL WHEN YOU WANT TO BLOW YOUR TOP

Make no mistake about it: maintaining composure in the face of a harsh opponent is hard. But there are two key practices we should hold up above all the others in this chapter.

First, tough tactics feel less threatening when we can recruit allies. Psychologists have found that when we are in the presence of a friend, hills appear to be less steep,[11] and we are less likely to give in to the views of people we disagree with.[12] Social neuroscientists find that the parts of our brain that become activated when we're under threat remain far calmer when we're holding someone's hand (even the hand of a stranger works, although the hand of a friend is better[13]). Even if we cannot bring someone with us to a meeting or negotiation, we can enlist that person's help as a coach or sounding board for talking through the challenge, and ask them to be on "standby" for a phone call during a break or afterward.

Don't hesitate to recruit this support. It doesn't reflect weakness; it's more like putting oil in an engine (in this case, our brain and nervous system) so that it runs better. Having allies helps us to think and act more effectively in stressful circumstances.

Second, if we feel overwhelmed or outgunned, it is often best to take a break and start over after we've had a few moments to think, cool down, or consult with an ally. Again, we might ask other colleagues or friends to join the meeting. We might ask someone (or hire someone) to come in and advocate or negotiate on our behalf, or hire a third-party mediator to help cool temperatures and create a more productive process. We might decide to break off the relationship and go to Plan B. When we feel we are losing control, it is better to stop than to improvise.

Threats become less threatening when we know we have an option or person we can go to in a pinch. Do a little work ahead of time to notify possible helpers, and improve your BATNA. It will help you feel there are options for changing or improving the process.

SHOWDOWNS VS. FLARE-UPS

Life isn't always predictable, especially when it comes to other people. It's always preferable to have time before a confrontation to think and to prepare, but what about the instant flare-ups, those situations where we are blindsided by someone else's words or actions?

The most important thing we can do is adopt the well-known credo, "First, do no harm." The easiest way to do this is to listen. Listening buys us time.

I've shadowed a number of senior leaders and watched them at moments of tension or conflict. Although they are typically action-oriented people, the wisest among them excel at giving themselves time to stop and think when they're becoming emotional, rather than winging it.

When we're feeling too intimidated or angry to continue with the conversation, use this kind of language to give yourself time to cool down and prepare:

- "I can hear that this is really important and I do want to work through it with you. I can't do it now, but can I call you later?"
- "I'm not sure I agree with you, but I do want to hear more. Let's set up a time to meet."
- "This is a problem we need to deal with together. Give me just a minute to take care of something, and then I'll come find you."

It is better to take some time to think and recruit help than it is to react in ways that we may regret, or that paper over the problem or issue. Even if the issue has to be resolved quickly, and we have to get back to someone in 30 minutes or less, we can always take a few minutes to think hard about what we want, what they want, what happens for each of us if we can't come to an agreement, and what suggestions we might make to try to resolve the problem.

With strangers and professional associates there are usually limits to how far bad behavior can go, because we're operating within the boundaries of appropriate conduct. But in close relationships we say and do things with fewer constraints, and there's greater potential for damage. In short, we need tools for handling conflicts with friends and family, too.

"I can take care of my enemies all right. But my damn friends . . . they're the ones who keep me walking the floor nights!"
—WARREN G. HARDING [1]

CHAPTER 7

Friends and Family

Resolving conflict in close relationships

CLOSE RELATIONSHIPS are like dense stars: they create their own gravitational pull, for better or for worse. When conflicts arise with close friends, roommates, lovers, teammates, and family members, they can pack an added punch.[2] That's because we're often not arguing about or negotiating a specific issue as much as we are revisiting emotional themes in the relationship. These might include a desire to be loved or liked, to be respected or recognized, or to have freedom in the context of commitments. They can include the issue of power – who gets to decide, or have a say? Whose views matter? Whether it's in the bedroom of a home or the chambers of city hall, conflict between people who know one another well can quickly escalate in ways that make negotiating more difficult, and avoidance and giving in more likely.

When I became a father, I felt cautiously optimistic about my parental abilities. After all, I was filled with immeasurable love and gratitude the day each of my two children was born; I had trained to be a psychotherapist and read many psychological studies and books on relationships; and I had treated kids and families and recognized the patterns that parents fell into. *I'll know what to do and say,* I thought.

The first time I yelled at my son, after a long day of whining and temper tantrums ("Just get in the bath! Right now!"), I was too angry in the moment to receive any coaching from my surprised wife, or to stop and think about choices. An hour later I had cooled down; I regretted my choice and apologized.

And yet I did it again, a week later. I was driving in heavy traffic and one child screamed at the other. "Quiet – now!" I yelled. This time I began to feel regretful and irritated with myself a few minutes later. I knew in the back of my mind that yelling was not helpful. I had still yelled, but I was getting closer to the goal of substituting a new habit for an old one.

A few weeks later my son and daughter were bickering (honestly, we do have a happy household most of the time!) while I was on the phone, trying to talk to a friend who had been stranded at an airport. I cupped the phone and raised my voice. "I am trying to talk to Dan, and in a minute I am going to yell. Okay?" My kids paused for a moment, and my wife swooped in and took over.

Our closest relationships bring out the most primitive, well-worn responses in our emotional playbooks. We get them from our genes, from our family interactions, and from observing others. Close relationships are contexts in which we tend to speak with fewer of the filters or rules we unconsciously use at the office or a dinner party where we don't know everyone well.

PROTECTING THE RELATIONSHIP

When we assume we'll be dealing with someone for a long time, protecting the relationship becomes the center of the conflict crucible. This raises four special challenges to our mastery, awareness, and poise.

Challenge 1: We become worse at problem solving

In the classic Warner Brothers cartoon of the same name, Chip and Dale (two extremely polite chipmunks) implore one another to go first:

"Please," says one, "I insist."
"No, no," replies the other, "after you."
"Oh, but I couldn't, really! After *you*."

This amusing dynamic points to what researchers have found: close friends tend to reach suboptimal outcomes when negotiating because both people simply concede without exploring options that would have left both sides better off.[3] We can understand this tendency if we realize that couples and friends often put their relationship and emotional well-being far ahead of whatever material outcome is in play. This leads to one person or the other giving in, in order to satisfice.[4]

While an economist might simply point to the total dollars or points that each side achieves, a psychologist will ask: How has the relationship been affected – will the people involved want to deal with one another again? Has trust been harmed in ways that will jeopardize or wipe out future opportunities to collaborate? Was the experience pleasant and rewarding? Or were people left feeling angry, disappointed, or humiliated?

After systematically studying hundreds of relationships over many years, psychologist and marriage researcher John Gottman and his colleagues found that the ability to resolve conflict is *the most important factor* in determining marital happiness and viability. As Gottman puts it:

If there's one lesson I've learned in my years of research . . . it is that a lasting marriage results from a couple's ability to resolve the conflicts that are inevitable in any relationship. Many couples tend to equate a low level of conflict with happiness and believe the claim "we never fight" is a sign of marital health. But I believe we grow in our relationships by reconciling our differences. That's how we become more loving people and truly experience the fruits of marriage.[5]

In close relationships the conflict crucible still has the same ingredients, but often in different proportions. For some couples, avoiding emotional upset is paramount, while for others it is a normal part of life and communication. (Couples, like people, develop habitual meta-emotional responses.) But social capital is always front and center.

Challenge 2: We bite our tongues

The second special negotiation problem in close relationships is that we don't speak up, because we fear losing or damaging the relationship. This is not crazy thinking. Close relationships are among the most precious resources we have; the quality of close relationships has been shown to boost health, happiness, and the length of our lives.[6] It is *highly rational* to fear initiating conflict if we believe that, as a result, we will lose the love, approval, or trust of a person who matters to us.

This is particularly true when we are dealing with someone powerful. Research shows that powerful people are biased toward action, particularly action that benefits them. When we depend on someone else for resources (a boss, a landlord, a mentor), trying to "make a negotiating table" can feel perilous. Powerful people typically have more and better choices than the less powerful, and therefore have less need for social capital. As a result, it's hard for us to find any leverage to encourage them to discuss a problem with us, so we're less likely to bring our needs or issues up at all.

The problem with biting our tongues is that it gets in the way of process mastery: we don't end up framing a *shared* problem or opportunity, because we don't disclose our interests or ask that they be met as part of an agreement. Instead, we avoid or give in, and while this preserves harmony in the short term, it can lead to resentment and emotional outbursts when our self-censoring begins to feel burdensome and unappreciated.

Challenge 3: We fail to recognize the real issues that are at play

Consider Susan's story.

SUSAN AND HER older sister have always had a difficult relationship. As kids they were competitive. Susan feels that Mara found ways to belittle her, cloaking her aggression in fake empathy. ("Oh, you didn't know about Tom's party? Oh. I guess you weren't invited . . . Um, sorry.") Decades later, Susan still feels on edge when Mara is around, particularly at family and holiday gatherings.

Now they are jogging together while Mara talks about her new car and her recent vacation. Then she asks Susan, "So, do you mind if Bill and I take the lake house this July?"

Susan feels herself getting annoyed and defensive. *She must know that we're struggling financially. Why would she ask for the lake house? They can go anywhere. Do they have to go to the lake?*

"Actually, we were going to go in July," Susan replies, breathing heavily as they turn a corner.

"It's just that you got the house last July," Mara says. "And I already talked with Mom about it."

Susan stops in her tracks. "Why would you do that?"

Mara replies, "Maybe because it's still *her* house?"

Now Susan's voice rises. "You went around me, and now you're asking me as an afterthought? Damn it, Mara, you are always doing this. You think you run the world."

Mara starts running again, her voice trailing off. "Forget it. You can have the house."

What is this argument really about? On one level, it is about who gets to stay at the family cottage in July. But that seems to be far less important – to Susan, at least – than their relationship as sisters. At this level, Susan is furious that Mara has seemingly gone behind her back, so that the request to discuss things, when it comes, is an afterthought. And at the deepest level, Susan feels that Mara is *always* treating her as an afterthought.

We all have our versions of "You're always doing this!" and those hidden issues can erupt when we are in conflict with a close colleague, friend, family member, or partner. Psychotherapy researchers Lester Luborsky and Paul Crits-Christoph call these issues "core conflictual relational themes" and describe them as having three components: our initial wish or intention; the imagined response of the other person; and our own imagined response to their response.[7] For example:

- Stephen wants to ask his sister to pitch in more with caring for an aging parent, but based on their past relationship dynamics, he imagines she will say no; then Stephen imagines how much he will resent her. This colors whether and how he will bring up the subject with her.
- In workplace meetings, we may expect that a proposal will be met with criticism from the boss, and we therefore prepare for battle in ways that make us defensive before the discussion has even begun.
- At home, a teenager pushing for greater autonomy from her parents may be ready to "pounce" emotionally when they assume that she will participate in family social plans.

Core conflictual relational themes tend to make us vulnerable to certain kinds of responses from people whose love, respect, and support are important to us. While we gain more control over our emotions as we age (finally arriving at a fully formed prefrontal cortex in our late twenties), adults of every age are susceptible to these kinds of core conflictual relational themes, which are really sensitivities to particular social and emotional threats (threats to status, autonomy, intimacy or affection, and self-esteem).[8]

Marriages are perhaps the central battleground for relationship conflict. In John Gottman's "Love Lab" at the University of Washington, researchers spent decades asking newlyweds and other couples to talk about a disagreement they had recently had. (Once left alone in the room, a couple typically didn't take long to get going.) But what interested the researchers was the emotional behaviors, and the patterns of behavior, that predicted marital satisfaction and stability. And this brings us to the fourth problem.

Challenge 4: We get stuck in downward spirals

When we've known someone for a long time – a family member, friend, neighbor, or close colleague – patterns of communication tend to emerge, like footpaths worn into a meadow. We slip into them all too easily, and while some patterns are familiar and comforting, others can dissolve our poise with frightening efficiency.

John Gottman and Jim Coan spent years devising a coding system that allows observers to label a couple's communication behaviors from second to second. Using it, they uncovered predictable patterns of communication that seem to occur across all couples. They found that some behaviors tended to worsen conflict, creating a "downward spiral." Some of the key codes from Gottman and Coan's coding system are described in Table 5.[9]

The most common pattern is the *criticism-defensiveness spiral*. This happens when one person criticizes the other, who then responds defensively – in turn provoking further criticism or defensiveness from the criticizer. Round and round we go, driven by emotion and accusation, ever further away from negotiating a solution to the issue at hand.

One unhelpful tendency in conflicts with friends or lovers is to create *wheels within wheels*. We move away from addressing the problem or complaint and instead name a pattern that we feel

TABLE 5

GOTTMAN/COAN COMMUNICATION CODES FOR DOWNWARD SPIRALS

CRITICISM BEHAVIORS Attacking character rather than a specific behavior	CONTEMPT BEHAVIORS Behaviors reflecting anger and disgust, intended to hurt	DEFENSIVE BEHAVIORS Rejection of blame, sometimes with indignation or sense of victimhood
Blaming: Statements that assign fault	*Insults and name-calling:* Shows of disrespect for the receiver through obvious verbal cruelty	*Denying responsibility:* Insisting that you are not to blame
Character attacks: Using "You never" and "You always" or making generalizations about the other person's behavior or beliefs	*Hostile humor:* Derogatory jokes; jokes that are only funny to the teller	*Excuses:* Claiming that circumstances beyond your control forced you to act as you did
Kitchen sinking: Laying out a long list of complaints	*Mockery:* Repeating what they've said in a way that makes fun of them	*Disagreeing with negative mind reading:* Disagreeing with your partner's theories about what you feel, believe, or want
Betrayal statements: Saying things that call into question the other person's trustworthiness (e.g., "How could you?")	*Body language:* Rolling the eyes, pulling the lip sideways on one or both sides of the mouth	*Cross-complaining:* Answering a complaint or criticism with a complaint of your own, often on another topic
Negative mind reading: Attributions about another's negative feelings or attitudes ("You're just saying that to manipulate me")		*Repeating yourself:* Repeating a position or statement over and over, without trying to learn more about the other person's perspective

By permission of Oxford University Press, USA. Adapted from Coan, J.A., & Gottman, J.M. (2007). The specific affect coding system (SPAFF). In *Handbook of emotion elicitation and assessment*, J.A. Coan and J.B. Allen, eds. (Oxford University Press), 272–275.

is occurring. "You know," we say in the middle of an argument with our roommate, "we always seem to get into this. I think it's because you don't trust me." Those of us who are higher in emotional awareness (women, on average) tend to do this more often than those of us who are less aware.

In moments like this we *think* we are rising above the conflict, or helping to untangle or contain it. But these moves actually pull us away from solving the specific issue at hand and foster (sometimes very intellectualized) criticisms and defensiveness in the form of one person's theories about another or about the relationship. If we're in the middle of a conflict, we must beware the impulse to analyze patterns or offer theories about what is happening!

Happy couples don't necessarily fight less than other couples. In fact, the frequency of anger in a marriage doesn't predict anything at all in terms of the happiness or longevity of the relationship. Some happy couples fight often and passionately; others tend to avoid conflict. It is *how we solve the conflict that matters.*

HOW TO HAVE A GOOD FIGHT

These four challenges – poor problem solving, biting our tongues, hidden issues, and negative downward spirals in the ways we argue – call for key moves that will help in the heat of the conversation. There are additional techniques that will help us act with mastery, maintain awareness, and summon poise. I'll share those in a moment, but first I'd like to describe three things we can do *generally* to help set the conditions for better, more productive conflicts with friends, roommates, partners, or close colleagues.

1. **Don't push.** Pick a moment when the other person isn't pressed for time or burdened with other pressures. Sometimes the best outcome is simply to make the other person aware there is an issue we

want to discuss, and to agree on a good time to talk about it. (My wife is nodding her head.)

2. **Start with a constructive frame.** Describe the conversation as a way to reach a good outcome together. If we've just had a terrible fight, we don't want to make that the focus or purpose of the conversation; we will only rekindle the fight. For example, we might say, "I know we're both ticked off about what happened last night. Let's think together about what we can do to keep Friday nights a fun time for both of us. Can we brainstorm for a few minutes about that?"

3. **Invent ground rules together.** Agree on a time to talk with a partner, friend, team, or spouse. (Don't push!) When we sit down together, ask what she would suggest as ground rules and thank her for her ideas. Don't criticize or evaluate. Then add our ideas and share *why* each one might be helpful. Then look at all the ideas together. Are there any you can both commit to? Any you need to discuss? The following are some ground rules that I've found particularly helpful with leadership teams and in my own life with my spouse, children, and friends:

- **The six o'clock rule.** When major issues or disagreements surface after work, agree that we will address them the following day. Never discuss anything important or emotion-provoking after 6:00 p.m. Why? First, because our brains and bodies are tired; we need to eat and sleep and unwind from the day. Second, launching into a difficult conversation when we walk in the door from work is not a good plan. Third, going to bed feeling angry or upset is a recipe for poor sleep and continuing conflict the next day. But do commit to a time and place, and come prepared. Breakfast or lunch together is a wiser choice, even by video or phone if necessary. We will sleep better and avoid flare-ups by not raising issues in the evening. (If you don't work a 9-to-5 job, your version of the rule should reflect this: address major issues or disagreements earlier in your day rather than after you've spent hours working.)

- **The always/never rule.** When we've known someone a long time and are dealing with what we see as a chronic problem, *always* and *never* can quickly crawl into conversations. Remember that others will likely feel statements beginning with these words are criticisms. Stick with complaints; stick with the present; make a specific request or propose a specific solution.

- **Walk it out.** Some of us have about as much enthusiasm for face-to-face "relationship conversations" as we do for root canals. One way to invite a friend or family member to a negotiation or discussion is to go for a walk or hike. There are three benefits to this. First, research suggests that walking can promote creativity, perhaps by activating hormones and key areas of the brain.[10] Second, talking side by side instead of face to face promotes a sense of *we* rather than *me vs. you.* Walking helps us listen without having to take in emotional expressions or eye gazes that might trigger unhelpful responses. Finally, we get to go for a walk or a hike! If we live near a park or wild space, all the better: time in natural environments (even less than an hour) reduces anxiety and improves thinking.[11] Even if no agreement or solution is found, we will have done something enjoyable together by going for a walk.

Timing, framing, and ground rules are all good starting points for managing conflict with partners and family. Here are additional key moves to navigate the four challenges we've covered.

MASTERY IN CLOSE RELATIONSHIPS

It can feel strange to consider building negotiation mastery with someone we consider a close friend, ally, or partner – after all, we probably don't want to cultivate a view of this person as our opponent. But for all the reasons we've talked about, learning to negotiate more effectively within our close relationships can actually strengthen our bond, as well as bringing more of what we both want into our lives. Here are some moves to promote more effective problem solving:

- **Listen and validate first.** Often when someone brings up a difficult conversation or problem he's had, it can be tempting to go straight into problem-solving mode. *"Why didn't you try this or do that?"* we ask. Many of us – and men especially – fall into the "fix-it" trap. But sometimes what our friends or partners want is simply to be heard and *validated.* They want us to know about the problem and their experience first. "Man, that sounds awful! Sounds like she was so rude to you," we might say. Or "You're right – traffic around town is ridiculous these days." Once they feel heard, they may – or may not – ask for our advice ("I don't know . . . do you think there's any easier route to take?"), and we can suggest something that might help. But going there first will often provoke defensiveness because our advice sounds like criticism, implying the person brought the problem or hassle upon himself by overlooking an obvious solution. In short, sometimes the best way to go fast (toward a negotiated solution) is to go slow, by acknowledging what someone is feeling. Once he feels heard, he may be more ready to entertain solutions.
- **Separate interests from options.** Conflicts with our friends or lovers often start when one person proposes something the other isn't prepared for, or doesn't like. Remember disciplined curiosity? In this context it helps to ask, "Why do you

like that option?" Do this before reacting or offering a criticism of it. Often this one move helps defuse a blow-up before it happens; we will be able to propose something more palatable that meets our friend's interest just as well.

- **Generate more than one option.** Her proposal or plan is one plan. Before arguing its merits, can we develop any other options, based on what is important to each of us? It's more powerful to provide our preferred option(s) than to push against hers. Are there any trades we could make, or ways to combine options (go to the country today; go to the club tonight)? If not, could we agree on trades over time that give us each what we really want (go to the country this weekend; stay in the city next weekend)?

- **Let it marinate.** If none of the options seems agreeable to both people, commit to coming back in an hour or a day, and go do something else for a while. Let the options sit for a while. We might think of something even better, or we might find that we're willing to bend toward a compromise. We might also find that our partner has a great idea now that she knows our interest, or has decided she's happy with our preferred option after all.

Moves to help us speak up

Speaking up can be the hardest part for many of us. To gather courage, try the following.

- **Seek social resources.** Remember that having someone as an ally, even a silent one, can be incredibly helpful. This might mean calling a friend and asking her advice about how to bring something up, but it can also mean sharing our anxiety with a friend who will sympathize with us. Just having someone listen sends our brain a powerful message: *I have social capital elsewhere! I can take a small risk.* (But one caveat: find friends and allies who don't also have a relationship with our counterpart in the story. Putting friends in the middle is stressful to them, and risky to us if they feel compelled to share what we have disclosed in confidence.)

- **Frame a shared problem and invite the other person to improve it.** A shared problem goes one step beyond a complaint. Often the complaint has to come first; if we try to formulate a shared problem, the other person may not hear clearly what we want. But once they have said, "Sure, we can talk about the air conditioner," we might say, "Great. I want to cut down on our energy bill while making sure the apartment is comfortable for you. Is there anything you would add?"

- **Complain without criticizing.** When it comes to raising an issue, it is important to be concrete and direct about the behavior or problem rather than resorting to criticism. Sometimes criticism can be delivered with a smile, "Maybe you aren't as worried as I am about the environment, but I wondered if we could talk about not running the air conditioning all the time?" That sounds nice, but it is a criticism (negative mind reading that attributes a bad attitude to the other person). Instead, just say, "Hey, I want to cut down on our energy bill, and running the air conditioner is preventing that. Can we talk about it?" We should be specific, focus on what we want, and say how the other person's behavior, beliefs, or proposed solution is preventing us from achieving our interest.

AWARENESS IN
CLOSE RELATIONSHIPS

Some negotiations involve "shadow negotiations" – undercurrents in the conversation that reflect underlying concerns or confusion about whose interests or ideas matter most, or how the conversation should proceed.[12] To help uncover hidden issues or dynamics under the surface of a conversation, try these moves:

- **Define the crucible.** When we feel hesitant about bringing up a problem in a key relationship, it is important we understand why. Ask questions like: Why does this issue matter to me? What do I really want? Is it about the issue or about the way we deal with these things together? Before the conversation begins, try to clarify (perhaps with a friend or ally) what is really at stake.

- *Anything else?* Remember the key questions to ask in any negotiation: *What? Why? What else? What if . . . ?* When a friend or partner brings up an issue, and particularly if he seems emotional, it helps to put aside the urge to respond defensively and instead say something along the lines of, "Okay. I got it. Is there anything else?" We have to ask this sincerely, of course. But if they are given a little more room, people will sometimes open up and share something that saves both of us a lot of time by getting to the heart of the matter. ("Yes, actually; I'm still mad about the other night.")

- **Pause to reflect.** After we've uncovered the underlying interests – what the other person wants – think for a minute about what we want. When we don't like a proposal, we often reflexively decide that we want the opposite. ("You want to spend a quiet weekend in the country? Well then I want to go to a ballgame and the nightclub!") Psychological *reactance* is a physiological response we have when we feel our freedom is being threatened; it riles us up and can lead us to try to reassert our autonomy. One solution is to ask permission to think out loud about what we want before we react or give an answer. (And if our partner or friend can't let us do that, we should go away for a minute or two and think about it.)

- **Watch out for downward spirals.** I mentioned downward spirals earlier in this chapter as one of the four special challenges to our mastery, awareness, and poise when we are trying to protect relationships. To expand our awareness as we prepare a negotiation or in the heat of the moment, it helps to familiarize ourselves with these key behaviors and their indicators, listed in Table 5, and try to avoid getting sucked into a downward spiral. Like any new habit, we might have trouble keeping all these behaviors in mind, and making masterful moves to avoid them, right away. But over time we'll be able to notice them more quickly, and will be able to interrupt downward spirals more often as a result.
- **Reframe conflict as a normal feature of relationships.** Conflict is frequent even in happy relationships, and some conflicts will never really get resolved. In fact, close to 70 percent of marital conflicts are over issues that recur repeatedly.[13] Accepting that conflict is normal, even healthy, can help keep us from becoming defensive or irritated as soon as it shows up, and can help us maintain a more productive mindset for the negotiation or conversation that follows.

POISE IN CLOSE RELATIONSHIPS

Our poise can evaporate like water off a hot pan when we're in conflict with someone we love or value highly. We need ways to stay cool when things begin to heat up, or when the other person says or does that one thing that drives us nuts. Here are a few techniques to try:

- **Recast criticism as complaint.** It would be nice if other people would start with a complaint rather than a criticism. But suppose he launches right in with "I can't believe you told Cathy's teacher we're looking at alternative schools.

That was really stupid!" Or "This is so typical of you." The best way to avoid becoming defensive is to try to understand his concern before we respond. To do this, we can make ourselves ask at least one question to uncover the interest that lies behind the complaint (for example, "Are you worried Cathy's teacher will treat her differently somehow?"). It's hard to do, but asking a question will help us zero in on the complaint, sidestepping the criticism.

- **Acknowledge without agreeing.** Another powerful move we can make instead of responding defensively is to name the emotions we're seeing or hearing, even if we don't agree with the argument or accusation behind them. Saying, "I can see you are upset" doesn't mean we agree with her perceptions, claims, or arguments. But it does make the other person feel heard and understood, which can help calm her.

- **Apologize first.** If she is upset about something we did ("You parked the car four blocks away last night, and it made me late for my meeting!"), we can apologize before moving on to problem solving ("I'm really sorry. Parking is a pain this time of year. What should we do so that this doesn't happen again?"). Sometimes the other person wants an apology more than anything else, and our efforts to explain our action or propose a new rule or plan can sound like defensiveness and pull the conversation toward a downward spiral.

- **Repair moves.** Making repair moves helps to soothe the other person, ease tension, and direct the conversation toward more productive terrain. Sometimes repair moves come out of the blue, as when a couple sits in stony silence until one cracks a joke or remembers something that they both enjoyed, producing a new positive feeling in the moment. Other times repair moves take several awkward efforts, sometimes by both people.

These four repair moves help *soothe*:

- Name the feeling ("Wow. I'm really disappointed.")
- Ask for help ("Can you help me cool down?"
  "Can I finish, please?")
- Use humor – say or do something amusing that releases
  tension (this could be a private joke or a facial expression,
  gesture, or phrase known only to the two of you)
- Reminisce – remember a positive memory together

And these two soothe while also helping to redirect the conversation:

- Problem-solve ("Could we brainstorm together for a
  moment?" "Could I explain why I did that, and then I'll be
  totally quiet and let you say your piece?")
- Create a shared complaint – *us against the world* ("You know,
  regardless of what got us into this mess, I just have to say:
  wasn't that hotel awful?")

Close or familiar relationships present their own challenges to mastery, awareness, and poise. Valued relationships add four challenges to negotiations: they cause us to be lazy problem solvers; they make us afraid to speak up; they cause us to miss the hidden issues that matter most; and they often get us stuck in downward communication spirals.

We need to watch out for these common obstacles, and learn to steer away from or out of them. We will get better over time by keeping them in mind (and sharing them with others who matter to us), but remember that nothing happens overnight. As we learned in Chapter 3, mastery requires practice. It may seem awkward to try new "moves" when we have done things the same way for a long time. We can pick just *one* to start, a new behavior that seems like it might have the most immediate impact on our relationship. Just as pulling one thread in a knot can sometimes undo most of it, we may find that trying one new move in our next negotiation or conflict can dislodge old patterns and open up new avenues in the conversation.

Handling foes and tough tactics isn't easy; sometimes handling conflict with family and friends is even harder. But what happens when we are asked to represent our family, team, or company in a negotiation?

You guessed it: new challenges arise. Not only do we have to deal with the other side; we also have people looking over our shoulder and holding us accountable. Leading negotiations isn't easy, but it's a tremendously valuable skill. And you can learn to do it with confidence.

"No good deed goes unpunished."
—CLARE BOOTH LUCE

CHAPTER 8

Leading

Negotiating on behalf of others

ON A HOT July night, fifty or so members of the Lakeview Neighborhood Association are crowded into the living room of Keith and Wanda Bradford. The mood is testy.

"Here's the thing, Keith: I don't see why we should give them an inch. What that developer is proposing to build is going to ruin this neighborhood. Seven stories?! Seventy to a 100 units? It's going to generate so much traffic! And noise! And who knows what kind of people might be moving in and throwing parties at all hours!"

A murmur of agreement ripples through the room.

Keith takes a deep breath, thinking about how to respond. "I don't like it either, Haley, but I don't know that we can stop it. We can fight the rezoning proposal so that they can only build 24 units. But they have the right to put up a seven-story building if they want to. Now, they seem to want to sit down with us on this, and the mayor and council have urged me to do that, to see whether there is at least room for compromise."

Now Cam speaks up. "I'm not worried about the traffic. What gets me is the height of the building. My garden will be in constant shade year round! I could live with 40 units if the thing were three stories."

"Live with it? Really?" Gerry stands up abruptly, his voice rising. "So, what – we just tell them that 40 units would be okay? I don't know . . . I think talking to them at all sends the message that this thing is going to happen. I still say we should pool our money and hire that attorney. Let's threaten to sue the council if they let the rezoning go through. Or sue the developer. That'll get their attention."

The room falls silent.

"I don't want to sue." Helen Tanaka's quiet voice surprises the group. "I don't want to spend our money on lawyers. That's not going to sit well with our friends on the council, or with other people in town."

A general din erupts, with people talking over one another and arguing about the best way to proceed.

Keith looks at Wanda across the room. She looks exhausted and exasperated – just the way he feels. Why did he agree to represent the group in the first place? It has been a thankless task over the last two months, and any way forward is certain to make some people unhappy with him.

IF YOU'VE EVER been called on to play the part of the "hired gun" at home or at work, you'll know that negotiating on behalf of others is very different from negotiating for yourself. When we are representing others in a dispute, the conflict crucible expands, putting much more at stake. We must pursue our ideal outcomes while our counterparts pursue theirs, *but we also* must consider the sometimes conflicting goals and priorities of those we represent. The social capital in play now includes our relationships with the people we represent *as well as* the ones we have with our opponents. Finally, we must cope with emotional behaviors that arise not only from our counterparts *but also* from our constituents.

It's easy to see why negotiating on behalf of others can be daunting. Sometimes we're given naïve instructions, such as, "Tell them to take it or leave it – but make sure they take it." Sometimes we're told to secure a deal that's unrealistic or nonsensical. And the personal or professional obligation we feel to the group whose concerns we share can be a heavy burden.

Mastery, awareness, and poise are still the keys to negotiating with confidence. But building and maintaining them in this expanded landscape bring a whole new set of challenges. The very first challenging task we face is critically important: before we can take our group's concerns to the other side, we need to get our people on the same page.

BACK TABLES

Making a table – agreeing on a shared problem to be solved together – can be hard enough when we have just one counterpart. But when we represent other people in a negotiation, more than one table is in play. In negotiation-speak, the group of people represented by an appointed negotiator or advocate is called a "back table."[1]

The biggest challenge we face when negotiating on behalf of others isn't even about getting what we want from the other side. The internal battle to bring our own "back table" into alignment is often far more onerous than the negotiation itself. When I coach negotiators in complex commercial or political environments, I hear a common refrain. "We struggle more than anything with our internal negotiations as we try to prepare for the external ones." People feel confounded by this. "It's crazy that we have the worst fights with our own side." My clients are often shocked when I tell them that this is typical and even normal. "I thought it was just us, and our dysfunctional team." Sure, group dynamics play a big role in how smoothly they'll come to agreement on what matters most; and some groups have healthier relationships and communication practices than others. But it's easy to see why there can be potential minefields throughout the process. Teams and organizations typically ask people (and pay them) to care about different things, which creates a predictable disagreement when those people are asked to describe what is "most important" in a potential outcome. And even if that weren't the case, all people on Earth see the world through their own eyes. As the group's representative, we will lead the negotiations with the other side. But we must also facilitate the preparation process of our side, which can be a tough negotiation in its own right.

MASTERY WHEN NEGOTIATING ON BEHALF OF OTHERS

When we're advocating for others in a dispute or negotiation, we need to expand our repertoire with a set of extra moves that help us wrangle a clear mandate from those we represent. We must:

- Clarify our authority
- Clarify the decision process by which our side will operate
- Gather information about the group's interests
- Avoid Christmas lists
- Convert concerns to goals
- Determine and agree on the group's priorities
- Set up a default decision mechanism
- Practice masterful communication with back tables
- Seek approval for an agreement

Clarify authority

When we're asked to negotiate on behalf of others, it is easy to assume that we are being given full authority to negotiate. However, this is rarely the case. It's essential to understand the kind of authority being entrusted to us, because in the heat of the actual negotiation there will be plenty of moments when we need to think on our feet and make decisions that affect the way the negotiation unfolds. We may want to reject a proposal in order to focus the conversation. Or we may want to declare victory and lock in an agreement with our counterparts after many hours of problem solving.

But if we take decisive action that our own back table is not on board with, or that it hasn't authorized us to take, it will cost us: both our counterparts and our own group will be irritated and possibly less cooperative in the next round. So we need to determine if we have authority to make the following moves:

- Propose new options
- Throw new issues into the mix
- Say yes or no to a final deal

It's essential that both we and our group are clear on the parameters of our powers before we begin. And the more authority we can negotiate with our group, the more likely we are to be effective at the table. Having to run back and forth between the negotiating table and the back table is time-consuming and can leave our counterparts with the impression that perhaps they would get more direct answers from someone else.

At one end of the spectrum, a fully empowered representative has had all authority delegated to her; any agreement she reaches will be approved and executed by those whom she represents. At the other end of the spectrum is a representative who has no authority at all and must shuttle back and forth to convey ideas, offers, and responses. You can imagine the potential for unintended confusion and offense if assumptions about authority turn out to be too optimistic.

Equally important to understand is the other negotiator's authority and limits in representing her group. We should ask her to clarify the kinds of authority she has before we begin the substantive negotiation.

SUPPOSE KEITH turns to the Lakeview Neighborhood Association and asks, "What kind of authority do you want to give me when I speak to the zoning commissioners?"

Some people might say, "I trust you to do and say the right things. You speak for me." Others might say, "Look, Keith, I like you a lot, but I really think the group needs to approve any new ideas or proposals that emerge in your talks with their side. Please don't agree to anything without getting the whole group to approve it first."

Keith is now facing an all too common problem in groups that are preparing to send someone to a negotiating table: it's not obvious who decides what, and by what process they will make decisions. In an informal, non-hierarchical group such as the Lakeview Neighborhood Association, it's not even clear who has the authority to grant Keith authority!

Clarify the decision process

In families, social circles, and organizations, a *strategic ambiguity* in authority often helps everyone feel important and save face. When you ask your organization, family, or team, "Who has the final say here?" you may have a fight on your hands. In an environment where there is matrixed management or other complicated structures, things can get especially messy. Companies – indeed, most organizations – have various people on staff who focus on different issues. If those people feel their interests are relevant to a decision, they may also feel they should have the right to force their negotiator to walk away if those interests are not adequately met.

But when it comes to preparing for negotiations, strategic ambiguity is risky. If, as the negotiator, we wait until the eleventh hour, when some sort of agreement has been reached or is close at hand, to clarify the decision process, we may have an internal fight that can derail or demoralize both sides, and provoke outrage in those who think we have acted unwisely or in bad faith. It is better to get clarity up front.

How should we do this? After all, if we come right out and ask, "Who has final say here?" we could be poking a very large sleeping bear and may set off a divisive battle of egos. Fortunately, there are ways to clarify the decision process that are less likely to provoke a confrontation. I use a "6D Framework" to describe the different decision processes that can be used by leaders and groups: [2]

- The leader **decides alone**, with or without input from the group.
- The leader **decides after consulting** with others in the group.
- The group **decides by consensus**.
- The leader **delegates** decision making to an individual or subgroup.
- The group **defers** making a decision to a later date.
- The group **declines** to make a decision.

I avoid putting anyone on the spot by showing this list to my team and asking for recommendations about which of the decision modes should be followed – or by proposing one myself.

As advocates seeking to help the group prepare, we should explain the different ways of reaching decisions and suggest which one makes the most sense. All six modes have their place, depending on the situation. For example, when time is short or the leader has unique knowledge to bring to bear, making the decision autonomously may make sense. When expertise or information pertinent to a decision is spread across the group, it might be better to decide after consulting, or decide by consensus. Once we have buy-in on how the group's input will be used, we'll be much less likely to set off unintended internal conflicts or experience challenges to our authority when the time comes to take action.

The key is to *be clear with everyone on our side about which decision mode is in use.* Ambiguity about who will reach the decision and how others will be involved can wreak havoc and destroy trust within groups and organizations. People often interpret the fact they were consulted as a signal that they will have a say in the final decision. They feel betrayed when the decision reached doesn't seem to be the consensus choice. For example, a CEO who polls his organization about where to locate a new headquarters office, then ultimately decides on the location that finished third in the polling, may find that he has created a firestorm.

Gather information

Once we have our marching orders, we'll need to create a plan for the negotiation and get everyone on board. One way to do this is to create a checklist to help the group start thinking like negotiators. The information collected will help us determine our CONA and then our BATNA.

FIGURE 4

LAKEVIEW NEIGHBORHOOD ASSOCIATION INTEREST CHECKLIST

- ❑ What will we do if we can't reach an agreement with the other side?
- ❑ What will the other side do?
- ❑ What are our goals and concerns, in order of importance?
- ❑ What are their goals and concerns, in order of importance?
- ❑ What information do we need? What questions do we want to ask the other side, or ask other stakeholders?

SUPPOSE KEITH brings a simple checklist, like the one in Figure 4, to a meeting of the Lakeview Neighborhood Association. When he starts asking members to discuss the questions on his list, the first obstacle he may encounter is skepticism about this kind of systematic approach. Someone might complain, "Why do we need to complicate things? Our goal is simple: block the building!" But this is a position, not a strategy. Keith needs to explain to the group why it's a good reason to prepare more systematically.[3] Keith might say:

> "Given what's at stake, I'd like us to take a rigorous and careful approach to preparing together."

> "I'd like us to set priorities together, recognizing that there may be some differences of opinion."

> "I want to be sure I push hard for what is most important to the group as a whole. There may be different views on that. Let's find out."

Even if Keith has a good negotiation process in mind, it may be wise for him to break it down into steps. At a first meeting he might ask the group to focus on what is most likely to happen if they cannot come to an agreement with the developer. Thinking hard about the consequences each side faces if there is no agreement (their CONAs) will give him some sense of how hard he will be expected to advocate for the Lakeview Neighborhood Association's preferred options. It will also help him enlist the group's imagination to create a better alternative to no agreement (their BATNA).

Table 6 shows a matrix that suggests general strategies based on what each side might walk away to. For each scenario it is critical we manage the expectations of our back table based on our

BATNA, the other side's BATNA, and our leverage. If the other side has a great BATNA to fall back on, we may have to work harder to raise doubts about some aspects of it, and to find new ways to create value for them. When our own side's alternative is poor, we mustn't forget that our opponent's may be poor as well. And when ours is great, we can't forget that the other side's may also be great.

When different people in the group perceive different consequences to an impasse, they will give divergent advice about how flexible we should be. A "deal-breaker" for one person may look like "a small price to pay" to someone else. Part of our job is not to be captured by the squeakiest wheel, but to arrive at a balanced view of what's most important to the group overall.

TABLE 6

STRATEGY MATRIX

WHAT DO WE DO IF . . . AND	THE OTHER SIDE HAS A GOOD ALTERNATIVE	THE OTHER SIDE HAS A POOR ALTERNATIVE
WE HAVE A GOOD ALTERNATIVE	Work hard to explore a deal that works for both sides; be prepared to walk away if it looks worse than our alternative.	Push hard for our preferred options while making sure the other side can defend the deal as fair, and better than their alternative; help them save face.
WE HAVE A POOR ALTERNATIVE	Uncover new interests and issues to differentiate our offer from that of potential competitors; work to improve our alternative!	Be prepared to work hard to invent options that create value and bridge differences; push for our preferred options but expect the other side to do the same.

Avoid Christmas lists

Another obstacle that can come up when we are preparing to represent a group in negotiations is the "Christmas list." If we seek input (or some other vaguely defined form of communication) from all members of a group, these people may then feel authorized to insist that all their aspirations must go into any new agreement. The naïve negotiator compiles a long list and says, "I'll do the best I can," which triggers another round of emails or phone calls from nervous individuals who want to be sure *their* priorities will be put first.

Negotiators in this situation are doomed. In the great majority of negotiations, they are not going to get everything they want – which means any outcome could be framed as a loss (compared to what was hoped for).

There is a better way. Having determined the decision process, we should cluster the long list of goals we have received into a simple list that includes the most important interests we think we have discerned, in a suggested order of importance. Then we can circulate this draft list to all members of the group. (Figure 5 shows what might be on Keith's list – things he has heard members of the Lakeview Neighborhood Association say are important to them.)

In most organizations, whether they are neighborhood associations or corporations, not everyone will agree on which interests are most important. In such cases, we may want to organize sub-teams focused on shared priorities to decide what outcome is acceptable and what is not.

To build or refine our list, we might ask these questions:

- What are the kinds of things that are most important to us?
- Why is each one important?
- What else is important?

People often reply to questions about interests with one word, such as *price* or *flexibility*. But to convert those vague leanings into

FIGURE 5

LAKEVIEW NEIGHBORHOOD ASSOCIATION'S
LIST OF INTERESTS

- Limit the number of units in the new development
- Limit the height of the new development
- Ensure that noise ordinances are strictly enforced
- Ensure that the design conforms to the neighborhood's architectural aesthetics

- Ensure that the building provides some commercial space
- Maintain ease of on-street parking
- Prevent crime
- Maintain property values
- Maintain a good relationship with city councilors
- Avoid negative publicity

something we can negotiate for, we need to create and test propositions that are more specific.

For example, price could mean:

- Reduce the unit price
- Minimize up-front payment
- Get a discount based on volume

Flexibility could mean:

- Make sure we can change the delivery date without a penalty
- Get a firm quote based on a hypothetical head count, to be adjusted once attendance is confirmed
- Get the right to swap our rental venue for the larger room if our event grows

Some people, when asked to describe what is most important, will tell us their key *options*, like "using eco-friendly materials." Again, *why* do they want what they're asking for? Are "eco-friendly materials" about preserving the group's sustainability mandate? (If so, will they be prepared to pay more if necessary?) Or is it about meeting regulatory requirements? (If so, what are the parameters that define "eco-friendly"?)

These underlying concerns are their real *interests*. Once you understand them, you will have greater leeway to invent various options that might meet those interests. Going to the table with only one option is a recipe for a tug-of-war, as each side pulls toward or away from it.

Convert concerns to goals

People who manage risk (like legal departments), or who are more anxious by temperament, may describe their interests in negatives rather than positives. "Don't agree to buildings more than four stories high!" "Don't rent any vacation house that is near a highway!" "Don't lose this client!" And so forth.

In this case, our job is to reframe negatively imagined outcomes as positive objectives.

"Don't agree to buildings more than four stories high!" becomes:

- Maintain our views
- Preserve afternoon sunlight
- Protect property values

"Don't rent a house near the highway!" becomes:

- Ensure privacy
- Ensure quiet
- Ensure safety

"Don't lose this client!" becomes:

- Keep our current scope of work, and expand if possible
- Maintain a good relationship with the client
- Avoid negative publicity that might jeopardize our reputation with other clients

Determine priorities

Once our group has produced a list of interests, we need the members' help to rank the points in order of importance. Why do this? Because unless we know which interests are more important, and which are less important, it will be very hard to make trades that create value.

Ranking can be contentious, because all members will be convinced their interests are the ones that ought to matter the most. In the case of the Lakeview Neighborhood Association, someone who lives closer to the proposed site for the seven-story building may be most concerned about its height; someone two blocks away might worry more about traffic, or property values.

With no clear right or wrong, it's up to us to ensure the decision-making process is fair, and that all the important issues are heard.

Sometimes we need to question or challenge assumptions or perceptions – respectfully, of course. That could sound like this:

"I hear you – I'm wondering also what others think?"

"That's an interesting point. Tell us more about what leads you to believe that?"

"My own view is a bit different here."

At other times we need to negotiate between two, or more,

group members who have diverging interests. We could say something like this:

"You are each pushing for the things you care about, which is great. Help me calibrate between your two lists. To be prepared I need to know where to push harder and be more creative, and where to show more flexibility."

"Potentially these are all really important interests. The hard task now is for all of you to help me understand which are *most* important."

Set up a decision mechanism

Despite our best efforts to reach consensus, it won't always be possible to have everyone happy with a ranked list, especially if the group is large and diverse, and members are passionately attached to their personal agendas. It helps to foresee this and proactively set up a default decision mechanism that we can revert to.

For example, in a family, if the kids can't all agree on what they want to do that afternoon, the default decision may rest with mom or dad. If the company's legal, engineering, and sales teams can't all agree on what is most important, the CEO may need to sign off on a final list.

After years of complaints from negotiators in the field, one health care company I worked with developed a "rapid decision team" to make final decisions about priorities and limits negotiators would work with if no internal consensus could be reached. The decision team accepted accountability for the mandate in each case; the negotiators' success was then measured against that mandate, rather than against the conflicting aspirations and interests that they were being asked to represent. By doing this, the company helped streamline the preparation process and provided negotiators with clearer and more useful guidance.

Practice masterful communication

When we represent a group, rehearsing small "bits" offers us the chance to get better guidance from the group. We may also find rehearsal useful for homing in on the right tone, or key phrases and messages, that our people want us to put forward. There are three places we may especially need rehearsing:

- The language to use for what we are proposing
- The way we will ask questions
- The way we will answer the likely questions or demands from the other side

In cases where group members have little patience for a more formal role-play, simply trying out language and asking for their reactions and guidance will help them feel heard and understood, raising their confidence in us as their advocate.

Of equal importance, these small moves can help them understand what we will be up against, and will give them a better sense of the challenge we face as their representative. "Be creative, tough, and articulate" is a starting point; we need more than that to make sure we are clear about how to communicate on the group's behalf.

Seek approval

When we believe we have done all that is possible at the negotiating table, or when our counterparts are truly prepared to move to their BATNA, it's time to bring a negotiated proposal back to our side for their approval.

Don't be dismayed if the proposal falls short of the ideal. Even proposals that are inadequate will be useful to test the group members' interests. Sometimes, as social psychologist Tim Wilson and I have noted, new interests and priorities can emerge in a person or group, or the importance of old ones can shift, based on new ideas or proposals that have been put forward.[4] Sometimes people don't know exactly what they want until they've been confronted with what they *don't* want.

When we seek approval from the back table, it is useful to break the task down into five steps.

1. **Remind group members of their interests and priorities, and of each side's BATNA.** Before we describe what has been put on the table, it is important we set the stage by reminding the group of its stated interests and priorities, and laying out again what each side (probably) walks away to if there is no deal. This is important because we will want to help the group evaluate the agreement in terms of 1) how well it meets their most important interests, and 2) how it compares to their BATNA.

2. **Explain the deal, starting from where they sit.** Just as we would take the perspective of a counterpart when thinking about a negotiation problem, we should present the deal by taking the perspective of our own constituents. Remember that they will have far less information or knowledge than we do about what actually went on in the negotiation. Research has shown that we often forget how little others know compared to what we know, and we assume they will understand our experience or ideas more easily than is the case.[5] So we should take the time to explain the proposal and the process that led to it; describe any steps we took to create value; and outline the trades or concessions the proposal represents. In other words, we should tell them the story that led to the agreement. This might seem an obvious step, but after long negotiations we sometimes forget to take it. Share what we learned about our opponent's interests, constraints, or future plans.

3. **Explain where things stand in the process.** What next steps in the negotiation have been agreed on, and which are up for further discussion? Is this a final offer, or is further negotiation possible?

For example, we might be preparing to respond with a counter-proposal. At this point, we need to explain what the other side has communicated in terms of its limits, and we should offer our views on whether we believe those limits are real. If we think this is the other side's best and final offer, we should say so.

4. **Make room for questions and doubts.** If we sound too much like salesmen, the group may worry that we have been corrupted in some way. If the agreement is reasonable, it's important we explain why. But we should also make room for lots of questions. And we shouldn't always be the one to answer those questions. We can say, "Well, what do others think?" or "I have a view on that, but I would like to hear from the group first." Back tables sometimes need to rehash points that seem ridiculously simple or obsolete on their way to reaching a decision. We have to resist the temptation to be "The Expert" on every matter. Group members will say many things we disagree with. The key is to help them avoid straying too far from a good process.

5. **Be prepared to make a recommendation, if asked.** Groups often have varying views on whether the agreement has merit, or should be accepted. In some situations we may be truly agnostic and look to the group for guidance on how to respond to the deal in hand. But at other times we may need to dislodge the back table from its fondest aspirations and wishful thinking, and prepare to make the case that the proposed agreement or decision meets its most important interests fairly well, and is likely to be better than walking away. Our recommendation may help the back table understand how we perceive the possibilities ahead. It will carry more weight if we show that we have thought through how well the current proposal meets each of the key interests our group has agreed on, and if we have prepared an argument that shows how the agreement could be described as reasonable or fair.

Note how many of these tasks involve taking the perspective

of others. Building mastery when negotiating on behalf of others depends to a great extent on maintaining an expanded awareness as we act.

AWARENESS WHEN NEGOTIATING ON BEHALF OF OTHERS

When we're leading negotiations, we still need to be situationists, thinking through the problem and issues from our side and the other side. But the landscape is more complex, because we have to consider the perspectives of both our counterparts and our back tables. Getting blindsided when we go to negotiate is hard enough, but getting blindsided by our back table can be even more stressful.

Manage egocentrism

In Chapter 4, we looked at how egocentrism can distort perceptions and impair judgment. Like so many other human characteristics, egocentrism can be exponentially magnified in a group, as people convince one another that their intuitive perceptions are true. This can take the form of groupthink, in which people reinforce one another's ideas and become closed to new information. Our people may get carried away by their notions of how badly the other side will want to reach agreement, or by dreaming up all the demands they want the other side to accept. Or a sense of panic or helplessness might prevent careful assessment of our options and what the other side believes it will walk away to.

As the process leader, we need to guard against this possibility by insisting on a rational and shared analysis of the issue and each side's potential walkaway. This might sound something like: "It's true we've got a lot to lose, but so have they. So maybe our task here is to think of how we might help the other side claim their idea of victory while also getting most of what we want." As their representative, it's our job to be the voice of reason and sound judgment.

Anticipate the Fundamental Attribution Error

In Chapter 4, we looked at our tendency to attribute traits or attitudes to other people based on their visible behaviors, failing to take into account their situation and its limitations. This Fundamental Attribution Error may be the most dangerous judgment trap for us as a group's representative. We can take it as a "predictable surprise" that our back table will seem to be unreasonable and rigid because of their strong interests and, potentially, their conflicts with others.[6] "Why can't they see the big picture?" we may wonder, as we try to navigate the two tables. It's important to put ourselves in their shoes: remember that they haven't been at the table with us, and they may not have thought through the problem and issues in as much detail as we have.

Meanwhile, they may see us as too accommodating. "Why is Keith always talking about the other side's interests and constraints? For heaven's sake, he's supposed to be pushing for what *we* want." We should expect pushback from our people when we have to explain that they can't get everything that they want. Remind them that we are on their side and want to help them meet their interests, but that we have to meet the other side's interests well enough that they will prefer to say yes rather than walk away.

Avoid false consensus

False consensus is another trap. Remember that we tend to assume more people will agree with us more often than is actually the case. When we make common cause with a group, particularly *against* something, we are sometimes surprised that others in the group have views of how best to go forward. It's important to solicit interests and normalize differing viewpoints early in the process, before the loudest or more convincing people in the room can claim that everyone shares their view. "I know we're all on the same team, here," we might say, "but I imagine there are different perceptions, different ideas, and different interests and priorities at the end of the day. It's really important to put those on the table so that I understand how to get the best possible result for our group."

Rein in self-serving biases

We also have to maintain awareness of our own bias, as the advocate. In some situations, a nervous negotiator may exaggerate the other side's power in order to set the stage for a "victory story" when a reasonable agreement is reached. In others, an advocate who is being paid for his time might unconsciously overestimate the likelihood of success in order to keep his paycheck going. Even when we are leading negotiations with good intentions, bias and overconfidence can skew our estimates of success or cause us to portray the situation as more hopeless than it might be.

Being aware of these tendencies – and talking about them at the start of preparations – can help protect us and our team from falling into intuitive System 1 thinking. To the extent that people have different perceptions, interests, or incentives, it is helpful not to demonize or dismiss them as narrow-minded or self-centered. It's better to come at the task as a kind of detective, prepared to ask lots of questions and test reactions to different possibilities. ("So, if they proposed 40 units and four stories, would you reject that out of hand? Why is that? Okay, and is that the only reason?")

Of course, not everyone is going to be reasonable, and as the appointed representative of the group, we are sometimes going to be on the receiving end of that unreasonableness. It can be a frustrating experience – which is all the more reason why confident handling of our negotiation duties requires that we maintain poise.

POISE WHEN NEGOTIATING ON BEHALF OF OTHERS

The techniques for maintaining poise described in Chapter 5 still apply when we represent others, but there are new potential triggers that we should bear in mind. For the most part, these triggers are related to the challenge of maintaining social capital with our back table, whether that is our family, our local softball team, our business unit, or our company or organization.

Feeling set up for failure

Although it is essential to clarify our mandate, adopt decision processes, and prepare systematically, those negotiating on behalf of others often don't take these steps. Why not?

For one thing, it can feel emotionally perilous to bring friends, colleagues, or allies together with the goal of eliciting and resolving different perceptions and priorities. After all, the group may include our boss, or our boss's boss (or friends of our parents, or important people in our city or town). They may be strong-willed people whom we respect and whose ideals we share. Some of them may not understand why we want to "complicate things" with initial conversations ("Just go and push for what we want!"). Even though we know we have the noblest intentions, it can be nerve-wracking to initiate a frank discussion that some people might view as confrontational or even disloyal.

For these reasons, most of us seek to soothe ourselves emotionally when we're asked to play the role of advocate. But short-term relief can cost us in the long run if these strategies undermine our ability to negotiate a satisfying outcome. We have to watch out for the following escape strategies in ourselves, as well as in those who represent us:

1. **Stacking the deck** (We describe the other side as impossibly tough and unyielding, while promising to do our best). This defense assumes that setting up a pessimistic expectation will give us room to shine if we gain a favorable outcome. The risk is that it may undermine the group's confidence in us, especially if we view every situation as "really tough" and every counterpart as "really difficult" – and it might undermine our own confidence as well.

2. **Self-handicapping** (We avoid preparing and opt instead to "wing it"). If the outcome is disappointing, we report back to our group that "in view of the limited time and limited input, this was the best I could do." Clearly, any emotional benefits from this defense come at the risk of producing a worse outcome.

3. **Asking for forgiveness** (We say yes to a proposal without adequately consulting the group, then ask them to please endorse what we have agreed to). This defense allows us to avoid confrontation with members of our own team, but risks making us seem untrustworthy and ineffective. The more experienced team members will have expected us to seek guidance from them about what is most important and where we might be prepared to make trades.

We can only use these strategies so many times before team members start to lose confidence in our effectiveness.

Feeling pressure to please everyone

We can use some of the moves described in Chapter 5 to lessen anxiety associated with the feeling that "everyone is counting on me," and with the possibility of provoking internal conflict. For example, can we recruit allies from within the group, or create an advocacy team rather than working alone? Pick a time of day for the meeting that will be most advantageous? (Hint: evening meetings are riskier in terms of mood and creativity, but good food might help.)

One of the hardest but most important jobs we have as leader is to normalize conflict in a group or organization while providing a process and framework for resolving it. Rather than creating a Christmas list containing everyone's favorite options, policies, or requirements, we should state up front that not everyone will get everything they want, and should push the group to prioritize its interests and concerns. This encourages people to think of different options that might be acceptable for each issue, rather than digging in around one. The idea is to get their buy-in to the process so we are not simply reacting to our own group's demands as well as the other side's. This also lets us explain key terms (like interests, issues, and BATNA) to our group.

Feeling stuck in the middle

Perhaps the biggest challenge to poise comes in the middle of a tough negotiation. Not only are we confronting demands, arguments, and constraints from the other side (along with criticisms and perhaps even threats), but we may be hearing anger, disappointment, or anxiety from our back table. We may be dealing with unproductive instructions stemming from our group members' emotions or lack of familiarity with the negotiation process. (Meanwhile, in more public negotiations, factions may be characterizing one another to the media or other outsiders.) It's not our job to play therapist, but as the leader of the negotiation we can and should help our colleagues manage emotions related to the experience we're all going through together. Here's how:

- **Acknowledge their feelings.** Our team wants to know that we are attuned to their needs and emotions, particularly when things get difficult. It helps to name what team members are feeling, even if we think their emotions are based on misperceptions or unreasonable expectations. We don't have to agree with their claims or conclusions; we just need to say what we think they are feeling. Accurately naming what people are feeling can help soothe them.
- **Name our feelings.** "You know," we might say, "I'm frustrated too. And I'm not sure how we can pull together here to propose something else that would be great for us, and possibly acceptable to the other side." Or "I'm exhausted from dealing with the other side all week, and I need your help generating some optimism at this moment about how we can get to a wise next step."

- **Refocus the conversation.** When we hear our people talking in terms of *positions*, *threats*, or *fairness*, try to reframe their arguments or advice in terms of *interests* and *options*. Ask the most vocal critics how they would improve the current proposal while still potentially meeting the other side's interests. Remember, our goal as negotiator is to help lead the group toward a realistic problem-solving mode, away from reacting to and criticizing the other side.

These moves are designed to help us avoid feeling "trapped in the middle" or "getting it from all sides." In many negotiations, this is exactly how we will feel. Even in lower-stakes deals, a single mild criticism from a boss – such as, "This seems like an okay deal, but I can't help feeling we could have done better" – might trigger feelings of resentment and disappointment. ("He really has no clue about what I went through to pull this off!")

COMMUNICATING WITH CONFIDENCE

Communicating effectively with our back table works best when we use language that is reasonably natural to us and to them. I've included some example scripts in this book as a jumping-off point, but you should come up with your own version of what each move would sound like. Think about the words or phrases that will resonate most, and have the most positive impact. Remember that practice – even on your own – is the key to communicating with mastery.

Also consider the format that communications should come in. Do you need to schedule a face-to-face meeting, or would an email chain, social media app, or group texting be more effective? Research suggests that face-to-face negotiations and conversations produce fewer impasses and provide more opportunities for learning than email does.[7] While it can feel less efficient – or more intimidating – meeting face to face makes us more accountable and inhibits our worst communication impulses. Just as the personal distance that a car provides can set the stage for road rage, email can encourage us to be less cooperative and constructive than we would be in person.

When we agree to represent a group, we are signing up to be criticized and second-guessed, often by people who are important to us. This can be very hard to take, especially in front of a crowd. Sometimes the best response is simply to stay silent. Remember, managing emotions and communication at the same time is difficult. It may be hours or days later when we finally find the words we wish we had used. (For example: "I definitely appreciate what Tony said yesterday. Nobody wants us to be stupid or soft here! But I also want to be sure we're being systematic in thinking about their proposal. Could I propose . . .")

Leadership is hard, but rewarding. Don't be demoralized by the frustration and effort that can come with the challenge of negotiating on behalf of others. This is a valuable skill that can help us contribute in a meaningful and substantial way to causes we care about. Remember, learning any new complex behavior will produce moments of discouragement and disorientation. What matters is what we do with them, and how we improve.[8]

Negotiating and leading are ultimately both personal undertakings. Chapter 9 will help you diagnose your own emotional, cognitive, and behavioral tendencies, and in the Appendix you will find tools to use as you build your negotiation practice.

Reading this book is a great start to becoming a more confident negotiator. Now begins the process of thinking about applying these ideas and insights to your own challenges.

*"Knowledge becomes wisdom only after
it has been put to good use."*

—MARK TWAIN

CHAPTER 9

You

Putting knowledge into practice

EVERY NEW beginning comes from some other beginning's end (an insight first expressed by Seneca the Younger, a famous stoic). And that's the purpose of this last chapter: to end this book by beginning your new, more confident negotiation practice.

It starts with you. As you begin your practice, it will help to take stock of your own tendencies so that you can keep them in mind. Knowing something about how you are likely to act, think, and feel across situations will help you think about the things you want to work on and the obstacles you need to overcome. If you tend to be more anxious, for example, or more impulsive, you can benefit by planning for it.

In Chapter 1, we looked at the power of confidence, and found that your comfort level with negotiation as an activity, and your expectations about how well you can do it, are the biggest predictors of your performance. Notice that this individual difference is about *mindset* rather than underlying personality traits (which is why you really *can* change how you negotiate without changing who you are).

In fact, most negotiation studies that put subjects with different personalities into particular situations have found that the situational factors have greater influence over how people will behave. Suppose you put people who are really competitive and really cooperative into a game where they can either cooperate or compete. You would expect their results to reflect their personal tendencies, right? But what if half the subjects played a game titled "The Community Game" and the other half played "The Wall Street Game," even though the games were identical in rules and incentives? Turns out the name of the game has a large effect on behavior, and the variation in personality predicts *nothing*. There is no difference in how the most and least competitive people behave. What matters is how people interpret the situation they're in.[1]

Of course, personality is a real force in our lives, and evidence suggests that over time it affects who we hang out with and the activities and situations we prefer. But humans – all of us – are also incredibly flexible in our behavioral strategies. We try to figure out and adapt to each situation we're in. This is why the best predictor of which friendships are formed in college is not personality but proximity (whether someone lives in your hallway or dorm).[2] What does this mean about your capacity to negotiate well? Again, your higher-level personality traits will have less effect on your outcomes than the mindset you adopt.

So as you reflect on your general tendencies and preferences, remember they are like an ocean tide, exerting a strong but hidden pull underneath your boat. It doesn't mean you can't drive the boat in lots of directions, and at different speeds. It just means that if you ignore the tide, you might find yourself somewhere other than where you planned to end up. Better to understand this hidden force and factor it in so that you reach your intended destination.

Being predisposed to feel negative emotion more often or more intensely does not mean that you cannot also have a lot of fun, feel optimistic at times, have adventures, or be effective in the world. Many historical figures have struggled with a tendency toward negative emotion (Abe Lincoln and Winston Churchill, for example). Personality traits are neither "good" nor "bad," but they can be adaptive or maladaptive in different environments.[3] Being prone to negative emotion might help you identify and escape a dangerous situation more quickly, for example, or empathize and connect more effectively with others.

Deliberately following key moves and practices in negotiation can also offset the effect of personality. For example, people who are more "agreeable" (kind and trusting) tend to concede more in negotiations when the task is to resolve a single issue, like agreeing on the selling price of a house. People who are highly agreeable (and those who are extraverted, too) do worse than the average person. But not much worse – that's the thing. Moreover, if friendlier, more accommodating types are taught to set a high goal for themselves before beginning the negotiation, the differences in performance disappear.[4]

So it is important to know how you go, but not because you are going to do better or worse as a negotiator. Rather, it is important to understand yourself so that you can predict where you might be tempted to cut corners in your preparation, where and how you might fall prey to biases and mental shortcuts, and how you may need to cope with difficult emotions differently.

ASSESSING YOUR TENDENCIES

Now that you understand how and why personality self-assessment can be useful – as well as recognizing its limits – here's a link to a free version of the Five Factor Inventory personality assessment tool: www.halmovius.com/resources.

Once you've completed the inventory and seen your results, take a look at Table 7 to understand how your trait scores might predispose you generally toward specific challenges or tendencies

TABLE 7

SPECIFIC CHALLENGES OR TENDENCIES RELATED TO TRAITS

IF YOU SCORED . . .	CONSIDER THE POSSIBILITY THAT . . .
High in Neuroticism	You may be more pessimistic, irritable and impatient than others (although see those subscales, specifically). Higher scores on *Anxiety, Self-Consciousness,* and *Vulnerability* tilt you toward looking for negatives and assuming the worst; *Depression* toward feeling resigned or incapable; *Hostility/Anger* toward expecting selfishness in the other person; *Impulsivity* toward acting or speaking without thinking.
Low in Neuroticism	Your emotional stability may not be shared by colleagues or others on your side. Their worry can be useful if it spurs you to prepare more methodically. You may worry less about avoiding negative emotion than some of your counterparts or colleagues.
High in Extraversion	Your counterpart may be less energetic and warm than you, and less direct in their communications and demands. This does not mean they do not value your relationship or the opportunity to work together. Likewise, someone's reluctance to discuss an issue with you does not mean that they dislike you or that the issue is settled.
Low in Extraversion	A person who talks a lot (or with great energy) is not necessarily trying to dominate the conversation. Clarify and practice asserting your needs, and make sure you have a compelling way to describe them. You can describe yourself as an introvert if you think it will help others to understand your demeanor.
High in Openness to Experience	You will be better than others at dealing with complexity and negotiations where multiple issues are in play. Your creativity and comfort with ambiguity may not be shared by your counterpart. They may want to move more concretely or discuss fewer options, and may not be comfortable with blue-sky "brainstorming" without some constraints or clear direction in place.

IF YOU SCORED . . .	CONSIDER THE POSSIBILITY THAT . . .
Low in Openness to Experience	You tend to see things in black and white, and come to conclusions quickly. Consider brainstorming with others to invent options for joint gain. If you're part of a team or group, try to include creative thinkers. Cultivate a stance of curiosity and remember that others may be less eager than you to move toward closure on each issue.
High in Agreeableness	You may benefit from setting more ambitious aspirations or targets for yourself, and from working hard to meet your own goals as well as satisfying the other person. Remember to share interests but not your bottom line. Predict that you may be quick to perceive violations of expectations about relationship and communication norms.
Low in Agreeableness	Others may truly want to reach a solution that is good for you, as well as themselves. Ask questions to discover what is most important to them. Beware leaping to conclusions about what they are thinking or what motivates them. Don't forget about the importance of maintaining healthy relationships, and be sure that your proposals will be considered "fair enough" that the other person or side will not be angered or insulted by them.
High in Conscientiousness	Your tendency toward orderliness and completing tasks might pull you deep into details sometimes; balance it with a focus on the big picture and remember that the perfect can be the enemy of the good. Accept that while you may want to proceed very carefully through a process, others may be less patient and want to jump to proposals or options. It doesn't mean that they are less invested than you are in getting a great result.
Low in Conscientiousness	Prepare, prepare, prepare. Even if you have a short amount of time, think about your interests and the other person or side's; think about the implications for you and for them of not reaching an agreement. Come ready with some options to propose. Don't be put off if they want to work in great detail; suggest a process that balances your level of attention or analysis with the amount of time available for the discussion.

when it comes to conflict and negotiations. Remember, these are general tendencies across situations; they don't predict your experience or outcome in a *particular* situation.

YOUR CRUCIBLES

You may find it useful to consider your general tendencies when you are defining the goals in your conflict crucible, as personality can predispose you to favor certain ingredients over time. For example:

- If you are less extraverted, less agreeable, and/or less open to experience, you may push more naturally to achieve material goals at the expense of building social capital. Remember the long-term value of good relationships and a solid reputation.
- If you are higher in neuroticism, you may worry more about avoiding additional negative emotions. You will also be more pessimistic than others about the prospect of achieving your material goals. Together, these tendencies can tilt you toward avoidance and giving in, rather than negotiating.
- Are you more agreeable and more extroverted? You may tend to prioritize social capital ahead of other goals, as relationships with others are generally very important to you. This can also lead you to give in too quickly or often.[5]

Remember, it is not only temperament that predicts our emotional life, but also our emotional awareness, our meta-emotional tendencies, and our coping styles. What we do with our emotions is up to each one of us. Being anxious by nature does not doom us to shy away from conflict, or to give in at the negotiating table. But it does mean we need strategies for dealing with that anxiety before, during, and after our challenging encounters.

Starting with a little self-reflection and some assessment of your own tendencies will be helpful. But practice matters too, an idea that should by now be firmly ingrained in your mind. No two situations are alike. So besides knowing yourself – and planning for your tendencies – your goal as you begin developing your practice should also be to maximize the likelihood that you will actually follow through and handle conflicts differently and better. To do this, you need tools.

In the Appendix that follows this chapter, you will find twelve tools to help you:

- Build mastery
- Expand awareness
- Summon and maintain poise
- Identify and handle tough tactics
- Manage negotiations with partners, friends, and family
- Clarify additional steps to take when leading
  negotiations on behalf of others

These tools are meant to help you prepare for particular situations, giving you a chance to think, feel, and act more systematically and with greater confidence. Remember, when it comes to change, trying new things really is the only way to get results.

You can find printable versions of these tools – as well as additional tools and exercises – at www.halmovius.com/resources/. On the same website, you can also take part in a conversation with others who have read this book, post questions, and share your experiences. Who knows? You and I might end up in a conversation.

JUST AS A university graduation ceremony is called "commencement" because the graduates commence a new life, so too, as you finish this book, you start something exciting: your new practice! If you shy away from conflict and negotiation, you're not alone. You are uniquely you, and you will create and resolve your own crucibles throughout your life. You can build your *resolve* by putting new ideas into practice that help you summon and maintain poise, expand your awareness, and increase your mastery in approaching and resolving conflicts and negotiations.

I have confidence in that!

And with practice, you will, too.

Appendix

Twelve Tools to Help Build Your Resolve

"A problem is a chance for you to do your best."

—DUKE ELLINGTON

BUILDING MASTERY

TOOL 1

DEFINING WHAT'S AT STAKE

DEFINE YOUR CRUCIBLE

Consider which of these matters most to you, and your objectives for each.

ACHIEVING MATERIAL GOALS:
In order of importance, what are my tangible objectives? (Financial, logistical, legal, etc.)

BUILDING SOCIAL CAPITAL:
What kind of relationship do I want with the other person? What kind of reputation do I want to cultivate?

MANAGING EMOTION:
How important is it for me to avoid feeling negative emotions?
Which negative emotions am I most at risk for? (See the tools in "Summoning and Maintaining Poise.")

DEFINE SUCCESS

Given how you've defined your crucible, what does success look like?
Complete the following sentence: "I will have succeeded in this negotiation if..."

If you are representing others, also complete this statement: "Given our interests and the consequences of no agreement, my team will feel we have succeeded if..."

TOOL 2

NEGOTIATION PREPARATION TEMPLATE *

CONSEQUENCES OF NO AGREEMENT (CONA)	What happens to each side if there is no agreement? What alternatives do we each have? How attractive are they? What risks does each side face?
INTERESTS	What are our goals and concerns? Among them, which are most important?
QUESTIONS	What do we want to ask them? (For example: *What is important to you? Why? What else is important? Relative to issues A and B, and how important is issue C?*) What might they ask us? How will we respond?
ISSUES	What issues might be negotiable? How can we break down potentially troublesome issues into smaller ones, (i.e., fractionate them)?
PACKAGES	What packages of options (one option from each issue) are great for us and possibly good enough for them? How can we exploit differences in what matters most to each of us?
ASPIRATIONS AND LIMITS	What might we propose initially, that we could argue for with a straight face in view of our relationship goals? At what point (on one issue or a combination of issues) would the deal be less attractive than what we could get if we walked away?
ARGUMENTS	What arguments most effectively support our proposals *in view of their interests and CONA*? What benchmarks, standards, principles, or precedents might be most compelling to them? What arguments might they raise?
TRADES AND CONCESSIONS	What might we give? What will we ask for in return? How should each side's BATNA affect our flexibility? How should the time or opportunities to negotiate affect it?

---

* I sometimes use the plural *we* and *our* in these tools so that they can be used with teams or groups. When you use the tools for one-to-one conversations, simply replace the *we* and *our* with I and *my*.

TOOL 3

NEGOTIATION PROCESS MAP

You've seen this map in Chapter 3, but I'm including it here so it is at hand as you work through the other tools. As you look at the map, ask yourself:

"Where am I most likely to get stuck? (What will my counterpart say or do to throw me off track?)"

"What can I do at those moments? (What does it sound like?)"

↑ ↑ ↑ ↑ ↑ ↑ ↑ ↑ → RESOLVE ↑ → → ↑ ↑ ↑ ↑ ↑ ↑ ↑ ↑ ↑

ESTABLISH	EXPLORE	INVENT	DECIDE	CAPTURE
A shared opportunity, problem or decision	Reactions to existing proposals	Options to create gains or bridge differences	Arguments (What makes this fair?)	Summarize what has been agreed
Key issues to discuss	Interests and priorities	Packages across issues	Closing trades, concessions	Define measures and milestones
Agenda: goals for meeting; timing; constraints	Areas of flexibility (If I... might you?)	Contingent commitments	In the event of an impasse: Do we walk away? Compromise? Bring in a third party?	Inform others affected by the decision
Who approves (or can veto) our outcome?	New issues (add, fractionate)			How can we do this better next time?

* LISTEN MORE THAN TALK *
* MONITOR TIME AND AGENDA *
* ACT WITH INTEGRITY *

EXPANDING AWARENESS

TOOL 4

CHECKLIST TO AVOID TRAPS IN THINKING

To avoid the traps of false consensus and overconfidence

❑ Conduct a pre-mortem

❑ Consider the opposite: What is the strongest case you can make for the other person's or side's view or proposal?

❑ Recall a time when you lacked power: spend five minutes thinking or writing about it

❑ Use a consultant to test assumptions, proposals/ options, and arguments

To avoid fixed-pie bias
Look for differences in . . .

❑ Interests (yours and theirs)

❑ Capabilities or resources

❑ Priorities (compare your ranking of issues to theirs)

❑ Time horizons

❑ Risk preferences

❑ Beliefs about the future

To avoid the trap of reactive devaluation
What is their likely proposal?

❑ How would you feel about it if it came from someone you respected (a third party) rather than the other side?

❑ Are there any ways it might be good for you?

❑ How can you improve it, rather than opposing it?

To avoid falling prey to the Fundamental Attribution Error
Ask yourself:
❏ How can I understand the other side's behavior, statements, or demands in terms of their interests and the constraints they face in this situation?
❏ Why might my counterpart be acting like a jerk? (Tough tactics have worked previously; has strong BATNA; is rewarded for this behavior; is under pressure to reach target; bad mood; needs to impress someone; other factors?)

To guard against helplessness/pessimism
❏ Conduct a pre-rebus: imagine the best outcome; how did it come about?

❏ Recall a time when you were powerful

❏ Seek support from a friend or ally

❏ Look for different kinds of power; remember that there is power in:
  • An elegant solution
  • A strong precedent, compelling example, or principle
  • Subject-matter expertise
  • A fair or transparent process
  • The ability to affect your counterpart's reputation or future dealings, perhaps in a coalition with others
  • Clarity: questions that can sharpen your focus and your mandate
  • Rehearsal
  • A positive mood and mindset

SUMMONING AND MAINTAINING POISE

TOOL 5

PLANNING FOR TEMPERAMENT

If you are high in **neuroticism** (negative emotionality), remember these powerful moves:

❑ Make friends with your tendencies; they're only trying to help
❑ Reinterpret negative feelings (e.g., anxiety as excitement)
❑ Recruit friends and allies (during preparation or to come with you)
❑ Be your own ally (use positive self-talk)

The other four major traits are less directly connected to difficulty in summoning and maintaining poise, but remember that being high in extraversion or agreeableness may predispose you to make concessions or accept a first offer more rapidly. To plan for this, focus on the tools in "Building Mastery" to ensure you have prepared thoroughly for negotiation.

TOOL 6

BODY AND ENVIRONMENT SCAN

BODY	ENVIRONMENT

Am I dealing with . . .
- ❏ Sleep deficit?
- ❏ Pain?
- ❏ Hunger?
- ❏ Emotional stress (perhaps from elsewhere)?

Try to . . .
- ❏ Get enough sleep
- ❏ Eat something in advance of the meeting (but not too much sugar or caffeine)
- ❏ Release tension through exercise

- ❏ Odor: Does the room or location smell bad?
- ❏ Noise: Is there noise that is irritating or distracting?
- ❏ Time of Day: Has it been a long time since a break, or food?
- ❏ Weather: Is the weather poor?

In the meeting . . .
- ❏ Use expansive posture
- ❏ Adopt a positive facial expression (to boost mood)
- ❏ Provide food if possible
- ❏ Take breaks

TOOL 7

META-EMOTIONAL TENDENCIES EXERCISE

To better understand your feelings and attitudes about your feelings, read through these lists of positive and negative emotions or feelings.

POSITIVE	NEGATIVE
Admiration for	Anger
Amusement	Contempt for
Attraction to	Disappointment
Gloating	Disgust
Gratification	Envy
Happy for	Fear
Hope	Guilt
Joy	Hate
Love	Indignation
Pride	Jealousy
Relief	Pity
	Regret
	Resentment
	Sadness
	Shame
	Worry

- Which ones are you most likely to feel as you approach this negotiation? (Make a check mark next to them.)
- Which ones are most unpleasant for you to feel? (Circle them.)
- For the ones that are both circled and checked, ask yourself: How will I cope with these emotions during the negotiation?

TOOL 8

IDENTIFYING EMOTIONAL TRIGGERS

Identify threats, criticisms, and demands that you anticipate hearing in the negotiation and analyze why these will bother you.

What am I afraid the other person will say (and with which emotional tone, if relevant)?

Why does it bother me? What does it seem to be conveying?

For example, you might be afraid the other person will say that you are "crazy." When you think about it, you realize this bothers you because it invalidates your goal and feels like the person is picking a fight. Or you might fear that someone will mimic you, which conveys a lack of respect.

Simply naming triggers and thinking about them will help you cope, but you should also keep the following phrases in mind to help you defuse the triggers:

"It seems that . . . "

"It sounds as if . . . "

"It feels like . . . "

TOOL 9

COPING STYLES QUIZ

This quiz will help you analyze how you prepare for a negotiation and whether there are other strategies you could consider using.

When I am nervous or despairing about an upcoming negotiation . . .

I try to distract myself by doing other things.

RARELY		SOMETIMES		OFTEN
1	2	3	4	5

I do things that make me feel better: e.g., eat, drink, exercise, watch a comedy, etc.

RARELY		SOMETIMES		OFTEN
1	2	3	4	5

I try to calm myself down through meditation, prayer, progressive relaxation, or breathing exercises.

RARELY		SOMETIMES		OFTEN
1	2	3	4	5

I vent to a friend or write about what I am going through.

RARELY		SOMETIMES		OFTEN
1	2	3	4	5

I talk to myself, reassure myself, and re-label what I am feeling in ways that make me less nervous or upset.

RARELY		SOMETIMES		OFTEN
1	2	3	4	5

If you scored 20 or above, remember to balance your emotion-focused strategies with problem-focused strategies.

If you scored 10 or below, consider balancing your preparation and problem-solving with strategies that help maintain a positive mood.

PROBLEM-FOCUSED COPING STRATEGIES

These strategies are most helpful when you can act to change the situation.

- ❏ Analyze the situation and make a plan
- ❏ Create the table by making a complaint or problem and/or requesting a meeting
- ❏ Gather and organize information
- ❏ Prepare to frame a shared problem
- ❏ Brainstorm potential solutions and packages to offer
- ❏ Prepare questions to ask
- ❏ Seek advice from others
- ❏ Practice (alone or with a friend/colleagues)

EMOTION-FOCUSED COPING STRATEGIES

These strategies are particularly beneficial when you can't do anything to change the situation.

- ❏ Distract yourself by doing other things
- ❏ Calm yourself down using meditation, prayer, progressive relaxation, or breathing exercises
- ❏ Vent to a friend
- ❏ Write in a journal
- ❏ Feel better through exercise
- ❏ Feel better through food, drink, or medication

DEALING WITH TOUGH TACTICS

TOOL 10

RECOGNIZING AND RESPONDING TO TOUGH TACTICS

This tool includes reminders of strategies to use when your counterparts are using the following tough tactics.

Extreme opening offers
- ❏ Inquire about fairness
- ❏ Counter with an equally exaggerated offer, then . . .
- ❏ Suggest a different process

Positional statements or demands
- ❏ Reframe/inquire in terms of interests

Anchors
- ❏ Put the anchor in context
- ❏ Disagree and refocus

Ultimata or threats
- ❏ Analyze CONA
- ❏ Reframe impasse as an option
- ❏ Get them to maybe
- ❏ Ignore it

Anger (signals a violation of boundaries)
- ❏ Take steps to ensure that you feel safe
- ❏ Acknowledge
- ❏ Separate the emotion from the problem
- ❏ Test by naming what you see and then ask them to share more about their feeling

**Criticism and disparagement
(suggests you are defective or blameworthy)**
- ❏ Don't take the bait
- ❏ Name and reframe

Contempt (blend of anger/disgust; communicates a lack of respect with sarcasm, mockery, rolling eyes)
- ❏ Reframe contempt as skepticism
- ❏ Ask for a complaint

Domineering (attempts to control the situation with incessant speech, invalidation, lecturing, etc.)
- ❏ Reframe the behavior (in your head) as defensiveness
- ❏ Signal that you have something to say
- ❏ Ask for the floor (to prevent interruption)
- ❏ Express anger
- ❏ Show up with allies

Disappointment (conveys sadness or dissatisfaction)
- ❏ Commit to silence
- ❏ Acknowledge and inquire

Personal threats
- ❏ Name the tactic and propose ending the conversation

RESOLVING CONFLICT WITH FRIENDS AND FAMILY

TOOL 11

CHECKLIST FOR NEGOTIATIONS AND CONFLICTS WITH FRIENDS AND FAMILY

To establish the right conditions . . .

❑ Don't push
  Pick the right moment
  Share issues in advance of discussing them
❑ Start with a positive frame: describe the conversation as a way to make life even better
❑ Invent ground rules together
  (see the examples on pages 130–31)

MOVES TO PROMOTE MORE EFFECTIVE PROBLEM SOLVING	**MOVES TO UNCOVER HIDDEN ISSUES**
❑ Separate interests from options	❑ Listen and validate
❑ Pause to reflect	❑ Anything else?
❑ Generate a few options	❑ Apologize first
❑ Let it marinate	

MOVES TO HELP YOU SPEAK UP	**MOVES TO PREVENT (AND ESCAPE FROM) DOWNWARD SPIRALS**
❑ Seek social resources	❑ Accept that conflict is normal
❑ Define the crucible	❑ Recast criticism as complaint
❑ Complain without criticism	❑ Offer a genuine apology
❑ Frame a shared problem and invite them to improve it	❑ Acknowledge without agreeing
	❑ Make repair moves*

---

* **Repair moves:** name your feeling; ask for help calming down; use humor to release tension for both of you; problem-solve; and create a shared complaint – us against the world

NEGOTIATING ON
BEHALF OF OTHERS

TOOL 12

SECURING AUTHORITY AND APPROVAL

To secure a clear mandate from those you represent:
- ❏ Clarify your authority
- ❏ Clarify communication ground rules
- ❏ Gather information about the group's interests
- ❏ Determine and agree upon the group's priorities
- ❏ Clarify the decision mode using the 6D Framework

To secure approval for an agreement from your group or team:
- ❏ Remind the group of their interests and priorities, and of each side's CONA
- ❏ Explain the deal, starting from where they sit
- ❏ Explain where things stand in the process
- ❏ Make room for questions and doubts
- ❏ Be prepared to make a recommendation, if asked

For more tools and resources, go to www.halmovius.com/resources.

Glossary

agreeableness: a tendency be trusting, compassionate, and polite in our dealings with others

anchor: a number or offer that psychologically "pulls" a negotiation toward a particular outcome or range of outcomes; this effect can be mitigated by a counter-anchor, which is an offer that doesn't respond directly to an initial anchor

awareness: cognitive confidence, or the ability to see situations and solutions wisely by using more systematic and deliberative thinking instead of just relying on the mental shortcuts

back table: the group of people represented by an appointed negotiator or advocate

BATNA: Best Alternative to a Negotiated Agreement; the most attractive (or least unattractive) course of action to pursue if no agreement is reached

claiming tactics: tactics in a negotiation that focus on dividing value or resources in a way that is favorable to one party at the other's expense; competitive rather than cooperative moves

claim value: push for our preferred option(s) at the expense of the other person or side

cognitive: related to intellectual behavior, such as thinking, reasoning, remembering

CONA: Consequences of No Agreement; the (sometimes complex and uncertain) outcomes that a person or team faces if they cannot reach agreement – understanding the CONA is a first step toward developing a BATNA

concessions: giving ground on an issue or issues

confidence: a feeling or belief that you can do something well (Merriam-Webster); a self-directed attitude focusing on the ability to perform well in a specific situation or context

conflict crucible: a metaphor for the complex and sometimes intense mixture of motives that are at stake when we approach conflicts, potential conflicts, or negotiations

core conflictual relationship themes: the internal, psychological conflict we may experience when approaching or imagining conflict consisting of: (a) our own wishes, needs, or intentions; (b) imagined responses from others; and (c) our own imagined response to that response

create value: moves or tactics that generate joint gains or "make the pie bigger" in a negotiation

criticism-defensiveness spiral: a communication pattern in which one person criticizes the other, who then responds defensively – in turn provoking further criticism or defensiveness from the criticizer

extraversion: positive emotionality or sociability, as well as a tendency to be outgoing

flinch: a physical reaction expressing disappointment or shock, often feigned by negotiators in an attempt to provoke an immediate concession

fractionate: to break one issue into several

Fundamental Attribution Error: the tendency to explain other people's behavior in terms of their personalities, attitudes, or intentions

Fundamental Negotiation Error: trying only to influence rather than create value

influence strategies: an array of tactics used to persuade someone to think, feel or behave differently, ranging in levels of assertiveness or aggression from pleading or arguing to threats and violence

making a table: agreeing on a shared problem to be solved together; a metaphor that refers to the bargaining table, where parties involved in a negotiation gather

mastery: behavioral confidence, or the ability to do something without having to think hard about what we are doing

meta-emotions: feelings about feelings; for example, when we see that someone is angry, we may be conditioned to feel fear and withdraw either physically or emotionally

mindset: a view of abilities as either fixed or changeable

mismeasurement problem: the problem that is created when only some things that matter can be easily measured

negotiation: a process through which people with conflicting views and goals voluntarily communicate with one another to try to reach a mutually beneficial agreement

Negotiator's Dilemma: the problem of inducing a counterpart to cooperate with us so that we can problem-solve together, without making ourselves vulnerable to exploitation

neuroticism: a tendency to more easily experience negative emotions, i.e., feel anxious, depressed, irritable, self-conscious, hopeless, impulsive

poise: emotional confidence, or the ability to be aware of our thoughts and feelings but not driven by them as we prepare for, carry out, and reflect on a difficult exchange

reactance: a physiological response that occurs when we feel our freedom or interests are being threatened; it can lead us to try to reassert our autonomy or to feel we want the opposite of what someone is proposing

reframing: recasting problems, claims, or arguments in a different light

relationship expectations: expectations about how we expect to be treated

satisficing: a term coined by Nobel Prize winner Herbert Simon, which means finding a "good enough" solution rather than the perfect one

self-serving biases: our tendency to think of ourselves as fair, competent, transparent, and virtuous

social capital: the trust and goodwill of others that we earn through good relationships and good reputation, and that we can draw on in the future.

System 1 thinking: a type of thinking that is intuitive and automatic, and that often takes place without our awareness or rational judgment

System 2 thinking: a type of thinking that engages in more careful searches for information, and more deliberate and cautious evaluation and planning

walkaway: what we walk away to if our negotiation fails (a BATNA, if we've identified one, or the CONA if we have not)

Notes

CHAPTER 1

1   Bolger, N., DeLongis, A., Kessler, R.C., & Schilling, E.A. (1989). Effects of daily stress on negative mood. *Journal of Personality and Social Psychology, 57,* 808–818.

2   Unpublished data from a survey conducted in June 2016 using Amazon's Mechanical Turk. The survey gathered responses from 338 adults (164 men; 174 women; 90 percent Caucasian). I asked people to rate the pleasantness or unpleasantness of specific experiences. On average respondents rated "Argue with a roommate," "Raise an issue with a friend when I believe it will lead to a fight or argument," and "Be sent to negotiate with unreasonable expectations about what can be achieved" as situations that were as unpleasant as "Attend a long, boring funeral on a hot day funeral," "Have my car break down on a busy street," and "Be stuck overnight in an airport with no place to sleep." (For more about MTurk see https://en.wikipedia.org/wiki/Amazon_Mechanical_Turk)

3   Larcker, D.F., Miles, S., Tayan, B., & Gutman, M.E. (2013). Executive coaching survey (The Miles Group and Stanford University).

4   See, for example, Stossel, S. (2013). What makes us happy, revisited. *The Atlantic* (May), http://www.theatlantic.com/magazine/archive/2013/05/thanks-mom/309287/; De Vogli, R., Chandola, T., & Marmot, M.G. (2007). Negative aspects of close relationships and heart disease. *Archives of Internal Medicine, 167,* 1951–1957; and House J.S., Landis K.R., & Umberson D. (1988). Social relationships and health. *Science,* 241, 540–545.

5   In the book *Crucial conversations: Tools for talking when stakes are high* (McGraw-Hill, 2012), Kerry Patterson, Joseph Grenny, Ron McMillan, and Al Switzler argue that the choice between relationships and outcomes is a "Fool's Choice." While I believe that there are ways to act constructively in the face of unfriendly behaviors (and will describe

them in the coming chapters), evidence also suggests this framing is too optimistic. It's not foolish to be aware of both kinds of goals, and to note that in some conflicts our counterparts will put one kind far ahead of the other.

6   I'm focusing here on ways of dealing with conflict directly, excluding methods that involve third-party assistance, such as mediation, arbitration, and consensus building.

7   Although measurement models often represent avoiding and giving in as distinct styles (see, for example, the Thomas-Kilmann Conflict Mode Instrument, or "TKI"), empirical studies have found considerable overlap in what they seem to measure. See Van der Vliert, E., & Kabanoff, B. (1990). Toward theory-based measures of conflict management. *Academy of Management Journal, 33*, 199–209. While Thomas and Kilmann went to some lengths to address socially desirable responding in designing their instrument, the TKI's own technical report (p. 8) suggests that avoiding and giving in ("accommodating") are the least socially desirable modes, reinforcing the evidence that these patterns of behavior are more prevalent than self-report instruments would lead us to believe. (Schaubhut, N.A. 2007. *Technical brief for the Thomas-Kilmann Conflict Mode Instrument: Description of the updated normative sample and implications for use.* CPP, Inc.)

8   Diekmann, K.A., Tenbrunsel, A.E., & Galinsky, A.D. (2003). From self-prediction to self-defeat: Behavioral forecasting, self-fulfilling prophecies, and the effect of competitive expectations. *Journal of Personality and Social Psychology, 85*, 672–683.

9   LaPiere, R.T. (1934). Attitudes vs. actions. *Social Forces, 13*(2), 230–237

10 Research by Kathleen O'Connor and Josh Arnold shows that relational concerns cause negotiators to set lower targets for themselves. See O'Connor, K.M., & Arnold, J.A. (2011). Sabotaging the deal: The way relational concerns undermine negotiators. *Journal of Experimental Social Psychology, 47*, 1167–1172. DOI: 10.1016/j.jesp.2011.04.004..

11 See, for example, Jang, K.L., & Livesley, W.J. (1996). Heritability of the Big Five personality dimensions and their facets: A twin study. *Journal of Personality, 64*, 577–592. Nevertheless, no single trait (or gene) has yet proven to be a very strong predictor of how people will behave in a conflict. It's important to remember here that traits are only one way in which individuals differ. (People also vary in terms of demographic variables, intelligence, abilities, and attitudes.)

12 Anthropologists and sociologists have noted that in extreme social contexts (e.g., drug cartels, gangs, the Mafia, dictatorships), violent force can be a primary tactic for enforcing rules; leaders in such environments may go out of their way to *ensure* that they have a dangerous reputation. When your main goal is not to be liked but to be feared, then violence may serve that goal. Even in such extreme situations, however, use of force is a risky strategy.

13 Schino, G., & Aureli, F. (2010). Primate reciprocity and its cognitive requirements. *Evolutionary Anthropology, 19*, 130–135.

14 Barnard, C., & Simon, H.A. (1947). *Administrative behavior: A study of decision-making processes in administrative organization* (Macmillan).

15 This definition summarizes an approach to negotiation that was inspired by three brilliant books: *A behavioral theory of labor negotiations* (1965); *The art and science of negotiation* (1982); and *Getting to yes* (1981). Chances are you're more familiar with the last one than the first two, but all three books helped launch the field of negotiation as a focus for both interdisciplinary research and a font of practical advice.

16 Rosenberg, M., Schooler, C., Schoenbach, C., & Rosenberg, F. (1995). Global self-esteem and specific self-esteem: Different concepts, different outcomes. *American Sociological Review, 60*(1), 141–156; Chen, G., Gully, S.M., & Eden, D. (2004). General self-efficacy and self-esteem: Toward theoretical and empirical distinction between correlated self-evaluations. *Journal of Organizational Behavior, 25*, 375–395.

17 Excerpted from an article by Gordon Edes. (2015). Dustin Pedroia delivers on scrappy attitude. ESPN website, http://espn.go.com/mlb/story/_/id/12916552/dustin-pedroia-rep-delivering-big-things-goes-back-college

18 Kruger, J., & Dunning, D. (1999). Unskilled and unaware of it: How difficulties in recognizing one's own incompetence lead to inflated self-assessments. *Journal of Personality and Social Psychology, 77*, 1121–34. A less well-known finding from these studies is that people who perform well often underestimate their skill compared to others. Egocentrism causes us to conclude that we are bad at hard tasks compared to others, and good at easy tasks, while failing to take into account that others probably also do badly at hard tasks and well at easy tasks. To the extent that negotiations in the real world can be a fairly hard task, most of us are likely to assume we are worse at managing negotiations than we actually are (relative to others). I discuss this in more depth in Chapter 4.

19 Livesay, H.C. (1975). *Andrew Carnegie and the rise of big business* (Little, Brown).

20 See, for example, Breckler, S.J. (1984). Empirical validation of affect, behavior, and cognition as distinct components of attitude. *Journal of Personality and Social Psychology 47*, 1191–1205.

21 In earlier drafts I called this component *judgment* to connote discernment. But achieving greater awareness is so central to the process of cultivating better judgment in conflict situations that *awareness* won out.

22 Todd, A., Forstmann, M., Burgmer, P., Brooks, A., & Galinsky, A. (2015). Anxious and egocentric: How specific emotions influence perspective taking. *Journal of Experimental Psychology: General, 144*, 374–391.

23 Elfenbein, H.A. (2015). Individual differences in negotiation: A nearly abandoned pursuit revived. *Current Directions in Psychological Science, 24*, 131–136.

24 Dweck, C. (2006). *Mindset: The new psychology of success* (Random House).

25 Kray, L.J. & Haselhuhn, M.P. (2007). Implicit negotiation beliefs and performance: Experimental and longitudinal evidence. *Journal of Personality and Social Psychology, 93*(1), 49–64.

CHAPTER 2

1   Galinsky, A.D., & Mussweiler, T. (2001). First offers as anchors: The role of perspective-taking and negotiator focus. *Journal of Personality and Social Psychology, 81*, 756–669.

2   Rackham, N., & Carlisle, J. (1978). The effective negotiator – Part I. *Journal of European Industrial Training, 2*, 6–11.

3   This term was coined by David Lax and Jim Sebenius (1987) in their classic book *The manager as negotiator* (Free Press).

4   Rackham, N., & Carlisle, J. (1978). The effective negotiator – Part I. *Journal of European Industrial Training, 2*, 6–11.

5   In multi-stakeholder contexts (e.g., commercial deals, takeovers, regulatory negotiations,etc.) there are also sometimes critical moves away from the table that can reset the issues, rearrange the parties, limit another party's options, or shut down a process. Two excellent books on this approach are Lax, D., & Sebenius, J. (2006). *3-D negotiation* (Harvard Business Review Press), and Subramanian, G. (2010). *Dealmaking: The new strategy of negotiauctions* (Norton).

6   See, for example, Karl, H.A., Susskind, L.E., & Wallace, K.H. (2007). A dialogue, not a diatribe: Effective integration of science and policy through joint fact finding. *Environment, 49*(1), 20–34; also Ehrman, J.R., & Stinson, B.L. (1999). Joint fact-finding and the use of technical experts. In *The consensus building handbook*, L. Susskind, S. McKearnan, and J. Thomas-Larmer, eds. (Sage Publications), 375–399.

7   Beckes, L., & Coan, J.A. (2012). Social baseline theory: The role of proximity in emotion and economy of action. *Social and Personality Psychology Compass, 5*, 976–988; see also Pennebaker, J.W. (1990). *Opening up: The healing power of confiding in others* (Morrow).

CHAPTER 4

1   For example, more than two-thirds of students in one MBA class estimated, prior to an upcoming negotiation, that their outcome would rank in the top quartile of the outcomes achieved: Kramer, R.M., Newton, E., & Pommerenke, P.L. (1993). Self-enhancement biases and negotiator judgment: Effects of self-esteem and mood. *Organizational Behavior and Human Decision Process, 56*, 110–133.

2   Ross, M., & Sicoly, F. (1979). Egocentric biases in availability and attribution. *Journal of Personality and Social Psychology, 37*(3), 322–336. See also Kwan, V.S.Y., John, O.P., Kenny, D.A., Bond, M.H., & Robins, R.W. (2004). Reconceptualizing individual differences in self-enhancement bias: An interpersonal approach. *Psychological Review 111*, 94–110.

3   Ross, L., & Ward, A. (1995). Naive realism: Implications for misunderstanding and divergent perceptions of fairness and bias. In *Values and knowledge*, T. Brown, E. Reed, & E. Turiel, eds. (Erlbaum). Armor, D.A. (1999). The illusion of objectivity: A bias in the perception of freedom from bias. *Dissertation Abstracts International: Section B: The Sciences and Engineering, 59*, 5163.

4   Babcock, L., Loewenstein, G., Issacharoff, S., & Camerer, C. (1995). Biased judgments of fairness in bargaining. *American Economic Review, 85*(5), 1337–1343; Babcock, L., & Loewenstein, G. (1997). Explaining bargaining impasse: The role of self-serving biases. *Journal of Economic Perspectives, 11*(1), 109–126.

5   Gelfand, M.J., Higgins, M., Nishii, L.H., Raver, J.L., Alexandria, D., Murakami, F., Yamaguchi, S., & Toyama, M. (2002). Culture and egocentric perceptions of fairness in conflict and negotiation. *Journal of Applied Psychology, 87*, 833–845.

6   Zuckerman, M. (1979). Attribution of success and failure revisited, or: The motivational bias is alive and well in attribution theory. *Journal of Personality, 47*(2), 254–287.

7   Hastorf, A.H., & Cantril, H. (1954). They saw a game: A case study. *Journal of Abnormal and Social Psychology, 49*(1), 129–134.

8   Vallone, R.P., Ross, L., & Lepper, M.R. (1985). The hostile media phenomenon: Biased perception and perceptions of media bias in coverage of the "Beirut Massacre." *Journal of Personality and Social Psychology, 49*, 577–585

9   Taber, C.S., & Lodge, M. (2006), Motivated skepticism in the evaluation of political beliefs. *American Journal of Political Science, 50*(3), 755–769. See also Stanovich, K.E., West, R.F., & Toplak, M.E. (2013). Myside bias, rational thinking, and intelligence. *Current Directions in Psychological Science, 22*(4), 259–264.

10 Kahneman, D., Knetsch, J.L., & Thaler R.H. (1990). Experimental tests of the endowment effect and the Coase theorem. *Journal of Political Economy, 98*(6), 1325–1348.

11 See, for example, Taylor, S.E., Kemeny, M.E., Reed, G.M., Bower, J.E., & Gruenewald, T.L. (2000). Psychological resources, positive illusions, and health. *American Psychologist, 55*, 99–109.

12 Stanovich, K.E., & West, R.F. (2000). Individual differences in reasoning: Implications for the rationality debate? *Behavioral and Brain Sciences, 23*, 645–726. The terms *System 1* and *System 2* were subsequently adopted and used more widely.

13 Ambady, N., & Rosenthal, R. (1993). Half a minute: Predicting teacher evaluations from thin slices of nonverbal behavior and physical attractiveness. *Journal of Personality and Social Psychology, 64*(3), 431–441. See also Malcolm Gladwell's (2005) best seller *Blink: The power of thinking without thinking* (Little Brown) for a review.

14 Berg, J.M., Tymoczko, J.L., & Stryer, L. (2002). *Biochemistry*, 5th ed. (W.H. Freeman). Retrieved from http://www.ncbi.nlm.nih.gov/books/NBK22436/

15 Clark, A. (2013). Whatever next? Predictive brains, situated agents, and the future of cognitive science. *Behavior and Brain Sciences, 36*, 181–204.

16 Galinsky, A.D., & Mussweiler, T. (2001). First offers as anchors: The role of perspective-taking and negotiator focus. *Journal of Personality and Social Psychology, 81*, 756–669; see also Sinaceur, M., Maddux, W.W., Vasiljevic, D., Perez, N.R., & Galinsky, A.D. (2013). Good things come to those who wait: Late first offers facilitate creative agreements in negotiation. *Personality and Social Psychology Bulletin, 39*, 814–825.

17 Ross, L., Greene, D., & House, P. (1977). The "false consensus effect": An egocentric bias in social perception and attribution processes. *Journal of Experimental Social Psychology, 13*(3), 279–301.

18 Chambers, J.R., & De Dreu, C.K.W. (2014). Egocentrism drives misunderstanding in conflict and negotiation. *Journal of Experimental Social Psychology 51*, 15–26. See also Thompson, L., & Hrebec, D. (1996). Lose–lose agreements in interdependent decision making. *Psychological Bulletin, 120*(3), 396–409.

19 Fukuno, M., & Ohbuchi, K. (1997). Cognitive biases in negotiation: The determinants of fixed-pie assumption and fairness bias. *Japanese Journal of Social Psychology, 13*, 43–52; Thompson, L., & Hrebec, D. (1996). Lose–lose agreements in interdependent decision making. *Psychological Bulletin, 120*(3), 396-409; Bazerman, M.H., Magliozzi, T., and Neale, M.A. (1985). The acquisition of an integrative response in a competitive market. *Organizational Behavior and Human Decision Processes, 35*(3): 294–313.

20 Allred K.G., Mallozzi, J.S., Matsui, F., & Raia, C.P. (1997). The influence of anger and compassion on negotiation performance. *Organizational Behavior and Human Decision Processes, 70*(3), 175–187.

21 Ross, L., & Stillinger, C. (1991). Barriers to conflict resolution. *Negotiation Journal, 7*(4), 389–404.

22 Moore, D.A. (2007). Not so above average after all: When people believe they are worse than average and its implications for theories of bias in social comparison. *Organizational Behavior and Human Decision Processes 102*, 42–58.

23 Galinsky, A.D., Maddux, W.W., Gilin, D., & White, J.B. (2008). Why it pays to get inside the head of your opponent: The differential effects of perspective taking and empathy in negotiations. *Psychological Science, 19*(4), 378–384. Galinsky and his colleagues have also found that the more powerful we feel in the situation, the worse we are at being able to take the perspective of others; see Galinsky, A.D., Magee, J.C., Inesi, M.E., & Gruenfeld, D.H. (2006). Power and perspectives not taken. *Psychological Science, 17*, 1068–1074.

24 Larrick, R.P., & Wu, G. (2007). Claiming a large slice of a small pie: Asymmetric disconfirmation in negotiation. *Journal of Personality and Social Psychology, 93*, 212–233.

25 Curhan, J.R., Elfenbein, H.A., & Eisenkraft, N. (2010). The objective value of subjective value: A multi-round negotiation study. *Journal of Applied Social Psychology, 40*(3), 690–709.

26 O'Connor, K.M. (2001). Distributive spirals: Negotiation impasses and the moderating role of disputant self-efficacy. *Organizational Behavior and Human Decision Processes, 84*, 148–176.

27 Galinsky, A.D., Maddux, W.W., Gilin, D., & White, J.B. (2008). Why it pays to get inside the head of your opponent: The differential effects of perspective taking and empathy in negotiations. *Psychological Science, 19*(4), 378–384.

28 Schaefer, P.S., Williams, C.C., Goodie, A.S., & Campbell, W.K. (2004). Overconfidence and the Big Five. *Journal of Research in Personality, 38*, 473–480.

29 Babcock, L., & Loewenstein, G. (1997). Explaining bargaining impasse: The role of self-serving biases. *The Journal of Economic Perspectives, 11,* 109–126; Whyte, G., & Sebenius, J. (1997). The effect of multiple anchors on anchoring in individual and group judgment. *Organizational Behavior and Human Decision Processes, 69*(1), 75–85.

30 Kennedy, J.A., Anderson, C., & Moore, D.M. (2013). When overconfidence is revealed to others: Testing the status-enhancement theory of overconfidence. *Organizational Behavior and Human Decision Processes, 122*(2), 266–279.

31 Klein, G. (2007). Performing a project premortem. *Harvard Business Review, 85*(9), 18–19.

32 Lord, C.G., Lepper, M.R., & Preston, E. (1984). Considering the opposite: A corrective strategy for social judgment. *Journal of Personality and Social Psychology, 47*(6), 1231–1243; see also Anderson, C.A. (1982). Inoculation and counterexplanation: Debiasing techniques in the perseverance of social theories. *Social Cognition, 1,* 126–139.

33 Galinsky, A.D., Gruenfeld, D.H., & Magee, J.C. (2003). From power to action. *Journal of Personality and Social Psychology, 85*(3), 453–466.

34 Research by Leigh Thompson has shown that past experience tends to bias us in future interactions with negotiators. See Thompson, L. (1990). The influence of experience on negotiation performance. *Journal of Experimental Social Psychology, 26,* 528–544.

35 Galinsky, A.D., Gruenfeld, D.H., & Magee, J.C. (2003). From power to action. *Journal of Personality and Social Psychology, 85*(3), 453–466.

CHAPTER 5

1 Leary, K., Pillemer, J., & Wheeler, M. (2013). Negotiating with emotion. *Harvard Business Review, 91,* 96–103.

2 Brooks, A.W., & Schweitzer, M.E. (2011). Can Nervous Nelly negotiate? How anxiety causes negotiators to make low first offers, exit early, and earn less profit. *Organizational Behavior and Human Decision Processes, 115,* 43–54.

3 Gross, R.W., & Levenson, R.W. (1997). Hiding feelings: The acute effects of inhibiting negative and positive emotion. *Journal of Abnormal Psychology, 106,* 95–103. See also Gross, J.J., & John, O.P. (2003). Individual differences in two emotion regulation processes: Implications for affect, relationships, and well-being. *Journal of Personality and Social Psychology, 85,* 348–362.

4 Trampe, D., Quoidbach, J., & Taquet, M. (2015). Emotions in everyday life. *PLoS One, 10:* e0145450. doi:10.1371/journal.pone.

5 Although we think of passion and reason as separate ways of thinking, that is not how the brain is organized: patients whose emotion circuits have been damaged (by stroke or other medical problem) have trouble making rational decisions. See, for example, Damasio, A. (1999). *The feeling of what happens* (Harcourt).

6 Beckes, L., & Coan, J.A. (2012). Social baseline theory: The role of proximity in emotion and economy of action. *Social and Personality Psychology Compass, 5,* 976–988.

7 See Adam Galinsky and Maurice Schweitzer's (2015) excellent book, *Friend and foe: When to cooperate, when to compete, and how to succeed at both* (Crown), which describes how flexibly we can adjust our strategies to different social environments and challenges.

8 Bolger, N., DeLongis, A., Kessler, R.C., & Schilling, E.A. (1989). Effects of daily stress on negative mood. *Journal of Personality and Social Psychology, 57,* 808–818.

9 By *goals* I mean here the material goals we are pursuing in an agreement. We always also have implicit goals, or goals that are unstated or unconscious – like being treated fairly, or feeling respected. Such goals are so common and so important that I am breaking them out into expectations about fairness and relationships. See also Roger Fisher and Daniel Shapiro's (2006) excellent book *Beyond reason: Using emotions as you negotiate* (Penguin) for a different and interesting look at implicit goals.

10 For more on this topic, see Tyler, T.R., & Degoey, P. (1995). Collective restraint in social dilemmas: Procedural justice and social identification effects on support for authorities. *Journal of Personality and Social Psychology, 69*(3), 482–497; also Tom Tyler's (1990) book *Why people obey the law* (Yale University Press).

11 Forgas, J.P. (1998). On feeling good and getting your way: Mood effects on negotiator cognition and bargaining strategies. *Journal of Personality and Social Psychology, 74*, 565–577.

12 For a compelling summary, see Wilson, T.D. (2004). *Strangers to ourselves* (Harvard University Press).

13 Baron, R.A. (1990). Environmentally induced positive affect: Its impact on self-efficacy and task performance, negotiation and conflict. *Journal of Applied Social Psychology, 20*, 368–384.

14 Egloff, B., Tausch, A., Kohlmann, C-W, & Krohne, H.W. (1995). Relationships between time of day, day of the week, and positive mood: Exploring the role of the mood measure. *Motivation and Emotion, 19*(2), 99–110.

15 Cohen, S. (1980). Aftereffects of stress on human performance and social behavior: A review of research and theory. *Psychological Bulletin, 88*(1), 82–108. See also Glass, D.C., Reim, B., & Singer, J.E. (1971). Behavioral consequences of adaptation to controllable and uncontrollable noise. *Journal of Experimental Social Psychology, 7*, 244–257.

16 Schwarz, N., & Clore, G.L. (1983). Mood, misattribution, and judgments of well-being: Informative and directive functions of affective states. *Journal of Personality and Social Psychology, 45*, 513–523.

17 Ibid.

18 Smit, H.J., Cotton, J.R., Hughes, S.C., & Rogers, P.J. (2013). Mood and cognitive performance effects of "energy" drink constituents: Caffeine, glucose and carbonation. *Nutritional neuroscience, 7*(3), 127–139.

19 Neckelmann, D., Mykletun, A., & Dahl, A.A. (2007). Chronic insomnia as a risk factor for developing anxiety and depression. *Sleep, 30*(7), 873–880.

20 Gatchel, R.J., Peng, Y.B., Peters, M.L., Fuchs, P.N., & Turk, D.C. (2007). The biopsychosocial approach to chronic pain: Scientific advances and future directions. *Psychological Bulletin, 133*, 581–624.

21 Carney, D.R., Cuddy, A.J., & Yap, A.J. (2010). Power posing: Brief nonverbal displays affect neuroendocrine levels and risk tolerance. *Psychological Science, 21*(10), 1363–1368.

22 There's some question among researchers as to the conditions under which posing has an effect. See Ranehill, E., Dreber, A., Johannesson, M., Leiberg, S., Sul, S., & Weber, R.A. (2015). Assessing the robustness of power posing: No effect on hormones and risk tolerance in a large sample of men and women. *Psychological Science, 26*, 653–656; and also commentary from the same journal issue. It may be that if you are aware of the effect of posing, the posing won't work. Still, it's worth a try – particularly if it gets you out of your chair!

23 Strack, F., Martin, L.L., & Stepper, S. (1988). Inhibiting and facilitating conditions of the human smile: A nonobtrusive test of the facial feedback hypothesis. *Journal of personality and social psychology, 54*(5), 768; Zuckerman, M., Klorman, R., Larrance, D.T., & Spiegel, N.H. (1981). Facial, autonomic, and subjective components of emotion: The facial feedback hypothesis versus the externalizer–internalizer distinction. *Journal of Personality and Social Psychology, 41*(5), 929–944. More recent research finds that "making faces" can also change patterns of brain activation: Coan, J.A., Allen, J.J.B., & Harmon-Jones, E. (2001). Voluntary facial expression and hemispheric asymmetry over the frontal cortex. *Psychophysiology, 38*, 912–925.

24 Brown, A.D., & Curhan, J.R. (2013). The polarizing effect of arousal on negotiation. *Psychological Science, 24*, 1928–1935.

25 John, C., Loehlin, J.C., McCrae, R.R., Costa, P.T., & John, O.P. (1998). Heritabilities of common and measure-specific components of the Big Five personality factors. *Journal of Research in Personality, 32*, 431–453; see p. 449.

26 Kapogiannis, D., Sutin, A., Davatzikos, C., Costa, P., & Resnick, S. (2013). The five factors of personality and regional cortical variability in the Baltimore longitudinal study of aging. *Human Brain Mapping, 34*, 2829–2840.

27 Watson, D., Clark, L.A., McIntyre, C.W., & Hamaker, S. (1992). Affect, personality, and social activity. *Journal of Personality and Social Psychology, 63*(6), 1011–1025; Fujita, F., Diener, E., & Sandvik, E. (1991). Gender differences in negative affect and well-being: The case for emotional intensity. *Journal of Personality and Social Psychology, 61*, 427–434.

28 McCrae, R.R., & Costa, P.T., Jr. (1987). Validation of the five-factor model of personality across instruments and observers. *Journal of Personality and Social Psychology, 52*, 81–90. See also Costa, P.T., and McCrae, R.R. (2009). The five-factor model and the NEO inventories. In *Oxford handbook of personality assessment*, J.N. Butcher, ed. (Oxford University Press), 299–322.

29 Larsen, R.J., & Diener, E. (1987). Affect intensity as an individual difference characteristic: A review. *Journal of Research in Personality, 21*, 1–39.

30 McCrae, R.R., & John, O.P. (1992). An introduction to the five-factor model and its applications. *Journal of Personality, 60*, 175–215.

31 Ein-Dor, T., & Tal, O. (2012). Scared saviors: Evidence that people high in attachment anxiety are more effective in alerting others to threat. *European Journal of Social Psychology, 42*, 667–671.

32 For an excellent read on how to be happier, see Haidt, J. (2007). *The happiness hypothesis: Putting ancient wisdom to the test of modern science* (Random House).

33 Mannor, M.J., Wowak, A.J., Bartkus, V.O., & Gomez-Mejia, L.R. (2015). Heavy lies the crown? How job anxiety affects top executive decision making in gain and loss contexts. *Strategic Management Journal, 37*(9), 1968–1989.

34 Brooks, A.W. (2014). Get excited: Reappraising pre-performance anxiety as excitement. *Journal of Experimental Psychology: General 43*, 1144–1158.

35 Beckes, L., & Coan, J.A. (2012). Social baseline theory: The role of proximity in emotion and economy of action. *Social and Personality Psychology Compass, 5*, 976–988.

36 One important move to make when seeking advice or a supportive ear is to explain our expectations for confidentiality. Talking to someone in our office who knows the other person well may make us feel better in the moment but could create problems later. It's often wisest to go well outside family or work colleagues if we want to talk about negotiations specific to those environments, and if we do involve someone who knows the other party, think carefully about whether he can realistically keep private what we might share in confidence.

37 Tod, D., Hardy, J., & Oliver, E. (2011). Effects of self-talk: A systematic review. *Journal of Sport and Exercise Psychology, 33*(5), 666–687; see also Dagrou, E., Gauvin, L., & Halliwell, W. (1992). The effects of positive, negative and neutral self-talk on motor performance. *Canadian Journal of Sport Sciences, 17*(2), 145–147; Raalte, J.L.V., Brewer, B.W., Lewis, B.P., Linder, D.E., Wildman, G., & Kozimor, J. (1995). Cork! The effects of positive and negative self-talk on dart throwing performance. *Journal of Sport Behavior, 18*, 50; Weinberg, R.S., Smith, J., Jackson, A., & Gould, D. (1984). Effect of association, dissociation and positive self-talk strategies on endurance performance. *Canadian Journal of Applied Sport Sciences, 9*, 25–32.

38 Zell, E., Warriner, A.B., & Albarracín, D. (2012). Splitting of the mind: When the you I talk to is me and needs commands. *Social Psychological and Personality Science, 3*, 5549–5555.

39 See, for example, Park, J., & Banaji, M.R. (2000). Mood and heuristics: The influence of happy and sad states on sensitivity and bias in stereotyping. *Journal of Personality and Social Psychology, 78*, 1005–1023; Isen, A.M. (1984). The influence of positive affect on decision making and cognitive organization. In *Advances in consumer research*, vol. 11, T.C. Kinnear, ed. (Association for Consumer Research), 534–537.

40 Barrett, L.F., Lane, R.D., Sechrest, L., & Schwartz, G.E. (2000). Sex differences in emotional awareness. *Personality and Social Psychology Bulletin, 26*(9), 1027–1035.

41 At the extreme, people afflicted with a condition called alexithymia have difficulty distinguishing between feelings and other kinds of arousal (like pain or hunger). Perhaps 8 percent of the population suffers from this condition, with equal numbers of men and women. See Taylor G.J., Bagby, M.R., & Parker, J.D.A. (1999). *Disorders of affect regulation: Alexithymia in medical and psychiatric illness* (Cambridge University Press).

42 Gottman, J.M., Katz, L.F., & Hooven, C. (1997). *Meta-emotion: How families communicate emotionally* (Lawrence Erlbaum Associates, Inc).

43 Ibid.

44 Van Kleef, G. A. (2009). How emotions regulate social life: The emotions as social information (EASI) model. *Current Directions in Psychological Science, 18*(3), 184–188.

45 Noonan, P. (2003). *What I saw at the revolution: A political life in the Reagan era* (Random House).

46 Lazarus, R.S. (1991). Progress on a cognitive-motivational-relational theory of emotion. *American Psychologist, 46*(8), 819.

47 Carver, C.S., & Connor-Smith, J. (2010). Personality and coping. *Annual Review of Psychology, 61*, 679–704.

48 Aldwin, C.M., & Revenson, T.A. (1987). Does coping help? A reexamination of the relation between coping and mental health. *Journal of Personality and Social Psychology, 53*(2), 337–348. See also Billings, A.G., & Moos, R.H. (1984). Coping, stress, and social resources among adults with unipolar depression. *Journal of Personality and Social Psychology, 46*(4), 877–891.

49 For a summary see Kelly M.M., Tyrka A.R., Anderson G.M., Price L.H. & Carpenter L.L. (2008) Sex differences in emotional and physiological responses to the Trier Social Stress Test. *Journal of behavior therapy and experimental psychiatry, 39*, 87-98.

50 Matud, M.P. (2004). Gender differences in stress and coping styles. *Personality and individual differences, 37*(7), 1401–1415.

51 Nolen-Hoeksema, S. (2012). Emotion regulation and psychopathology: The role of gender. *Annual Review of Clinical Psychology, 8*, 161–187.

52 Powers, S.I., Pietromonaco, P.R., Gunlicks, M., & Sayer, A. (2006). Dating couples' attachment styles and patterns of cortisol reactivity and recovery in response to a relationship conflict. *Journal of Personality and Social Psychology, 90*, 613–628.

53 For more on this very rich and interesting topic, see Helgeson, V.S. (2012). Gender, Stress, and Coping. In *The Oxford handbook of stress, health, and coping*, Ed. Folkman, Susan. Oxford University Press, 63-85; Christensen, A., & Heavey, C. L. (1990). Gender and social structure in demand-withdraw pattern of marital conflict. *Journal of Personality and Social Psychology, 59*, 73–81; Kiecolt-Glaser, J. K., & Newton, T. (2001). Marriage and health: His and hers. *Psychological Bulletin, 127*, 472–503.

CHAPTER 6

1   Fisher, R., & Ury, W.L. (1981). *Getting to yes: Negotiating agreement without giving in* (Penguin), 19–41.

2   Ury, W. (2007). *The power of a positive no* (Bantam Books).

3   Ordóñez, L.D., Schweitzer, M.E., Galinsky, A.D., & Bazerman, M.H. (2009). Goals gone wild: The systematic side effects of overprescribing goal setting, *Academy of Management Perspectives, 23*(3), 82–87.

4   Thomas, K.W., & Thomas, G.F. (2008). Conflict styles of men and women at six organization levels. *International Journal of Conflict Management, 19*, 148–166.

5   Piff, P.K., Kraus, M.W., Côté, S., Cheng, B.H., & Keltner, D. (2010). Having less, giving more: The influence of social class on prosocial behavior. *Journal of Personality and Social Psychology, 99*(5), 771–784.

6   Galinsky, A.D., Magee, J.C., Inesi, M.E., & Gruenfeld, D.H. (2006). Power and perspectives not taken. *Psychological Science, 17*, 1068–1074.

7   Van Kleef, G.A., De Dreu, C.K.W., Pietroni, D., & Manstead, A.S.R. (2006). Power and emotion in negotiation: Power moderates the interpersonal effects of anger and happiness on concession making. *European Journal of Social Psychology, 36*, 557–581. See also Sinaceur, M., & Tiedens, L.Z. (2006). Get mad and get more than even: When and why anger expression is effective in negotiations. *Journal of Experimental Social Psychology, 42*, 314–322.

8   In Western culture, where individualism is emphasized, anger is more often expressed by people with lower status. In collectivist cultures, like Japan, it is more often expressed by those with greater status. Perhaps this difference reflects the purpose of anger: in the West, individuals use it to express violations of personal freedom or fairness; in cultures like Japan it is used to signal violations of group norms or expectations. See Park, J., Kitayama, S., Markus, H.R., Coe, C.L., Miyamoto, Y., Karasawa, M., et al (2013). Social status and anger expression: The cultural moderation hypothesis. *Emotion, 13*, 1122–1131.

9   Gottman summarizes this research in Gottman, J.M., & Silver, N. (1999). *The seven principles for making marriage work* (Harmony).

10 Gottman, J.M., & Silver, N. (1999). *The seven principles for making marriage work* (Harmony).

11 Schnall, S., Harber, K.D., Stefanucci, J.K., & Proffitt, D.R. (2008). Social support and the perception of geographical slant. *Journal of Experimental Social Psychology, 44*, 1246–1255.

12 Asch, S.E. (1955). Opinions and social pressure. *Scientific American, 193*, 33–35.

13 Beckes, L., & Coan, J.A. (2012). Social baseline theory: The role of proximity in emotion and economy of action. *Social and Personality Psychology Compass, 5*, 976–988.

CHAPTER 7

1   A remark by Harding to editor William Alan White, quoted in Thomas Harry Williams et al. (1959). *A History of the United States* (Knopf).

2   Halevy, N., Chou, E., & Galinsky, A. (2012). Exhausting or exhilarating? Conflict as threat to interests, relationships and identities. *Journal of Experimental Social Psychology, 48*, 530–537.

3   Curhan. J.R., Neale, M.A., Ross, L., & Rosencranz-Engelmann, J. (2008). Relational accommodation in negotiation: Effects of egalitarianism and gender on economic efficiency and relational capital. *Organizational Behavior and Human Decision Processes, 107*, 192–205. See also Fry, W.R., Firestone, I.J., & Williams, D.L. (1983). Negotiation process and outcome of stranger dyads and dating couples: Do lovers lose? *Basic and Applied Social Psychology, 4*, 1–16.

4   Curhan. J.R., Neale, M.A., Ross, L., & Rosencranz-Engelmann, J. (2008). Relational accommodation in negotiation: Effects of egalitarianism and gender on economic efficiency and relational capital. *Organizational Behavior and Human Decision Processes, 107*, 192–205. See also Ross, L., & Ward, A. (1995). Psychological barriers to dispute resolution. *Advances in Experimental Social Psychology, 27*, 255–304.

5   Gottman, J.M., & Silver, N. (1994). What makes marriage work? *Psychology Today* (March), https://www.psychologytoday.com/articles/200910/what-makes-marriage-work

6   See House J.S., Landis K.R., & Umberson D. (1988). Social relationships and health. *Science, 241*, 540–545; Stossel, S. (2013). What makes us happy, revisited. *The Atlantic* (May), http://www.theatlantic.com/magazine/archive/2013/05/thanks-mom/309287/

7   Barber, J.P., Luborsky, L., Crits-Christoph, P., & Diguer, L. (1995). A comparison of core conflictual relationship themes before psychotherapy and during early sessions. *Journal of Consulting and Clinical Psychology, 63*(1), 145–148.). The Core Conflictual Relationship Theme coding system breaks down interpersonal patterns or conflict into components: (a) wishes, needs, or intentions expressed by the subject; (b) expected or actual responses from others; and (c) responses of self, i.e., the patient's own emotional, behavioral, or symptomatic responses to others' responses.

8   See also Fisher, R., & Shapiro, D. (2005). *Beyond reason: Using emotions as you negotiate* (Penguin) for a thoughtful discussion of what they call "core concerns."

9   Coan, J.A., & Gottman, J.M. (2007). The specific affect coding system (SPAFF). In *Handbook of emotion elicitation and assessment*, J.A. Coan and J.B. Allen, eds. (Oxford University Press), 267–285.

10 Oppezzo, M., & Schwartz, D.L. (2014). Give your ideas some legs: The positive effect of walking on creative thinking. *Journal of Experimental Psychology: Learning, Memory, and Cognition, 40*(4), 1142–1152. On the other hand, if you are already fairly anxious, you may want to stay put: Brown, A.D., & Curhan, J.R. (2013). The polarizing effect of arousal on negotiation. *Psychological Science, 24*, 1928–1935.

11 Bratman, G.N., Daily, G.C., Levy, B.J., & Gross, J.J. (2015). The benefits of nature experience: Improved affect and cognition. *Landscape and Urban Planning, 138*, 41–50.

12 The term *shadow negotiation* was coined by Deborah Kolb and Judith Williams (2000) in their book *The shadow negotiation: How women can master the hidden agendas that determine bargaining* (Simon and Schuster).

13 Gottman, J. (2016). Debunking 12 myths about relationships. Blog post on the Gottman Institute website, https://www.gottman.com/blog/debunking-12-myths-about-relationships/

CHAPTER 8

1   I believe this term was first coined by Roger Fisher (1969) in the book *International Conflict for Beginners* (Harper and Row).

2   My 6D Framework is based on a decision framework originally developed by management professors Victor Vroom and Arthur Jago. See Vroom, V.H., & Yetton, P.W. (1973). *Leadership and decision-making* (University of Pittsburgh Press).

3   An alternative approach to building consensus in community decisions is described in Susskind, L.E., & Cruikshank, J.L. (2006). *Breaking Robert's Rules: The new way to run your meeting, build consensus, and get results* (Oxford University Press).

4   Movius, H., & Wilson, T.D. (2011). How we feel about the deal. *Negotiation Journal, 27*(2), 241–250.

5   Camerer, C., Loewenstein, G., & Weber, M. (1989). The curse of knowledge in economic settings: An experimental analysis. *Journal of Political Economy, 97*(5), 1232–1254.

6   Bazerman, M.H., & Watkins, M.D. (2004). *Predictable surprises: The disasters you should have seen coming, and how to prevent them* (Harvard Business Review Press).

7   Thompson, L., & Nadler, J. (2002). Negotiating via information technology: Theory and application. *Journal of Social Issues, 58*(1), 109–124.

8   For a more extensive treatment of many of the challenges touched on in this chapter, see the book *Negotiating on Behalf of Others*, edited by Lawrence Susskind and Robert Mnookin (1999, Sage Press)

CHAPTER 9

1   Ross, L., & Ward, A. (1995). Psychological barriers to dispute resolution. *Advances in Experimental Social Psychology, 27*, 255–304.

2   Newcomb, T.M. (1960). Varieties of interpersonal attraction. In *Group dynamics: Research and theory*, 2nd ed., D. Cartwright and A. Zander, eds. (Row, Peterson), 104–119. See also Festinger, L., Schachter, S., & Bach, K. (1950). *Social pressures in informal groups* (Harper).

3   Penke, L., & Markus, J. (2016). The evolutionary genetics of personality revisited. *Current Opinion in Psychology, 7*, 104–109.

4   Barry, B., Friedman, R.A., & Smith, C. (1998). Bargainer characteristics in distributive and integrative negotiation. *Journal of Personality and Social Psychology, 74*, 345–359; see also Ma, Z., & Jaeger, A. (2005). Getting to yes in China: Exploring personality effects in Chinese negotiation styles. *Group Decision and Negotiation, 14*, 415–437.

5   Barry, B., Friedman, R.A., & Smith, C. (1998). Bargainer characteristics in distributive and integrative negotiation. *Journal of Personality and Social Psychology, 74*, 345–359.

Index

Figures and tables indicated by page numbers in italics.